T0328451

Cambridge Elements ≡

Elements in Research Methods for Developmental Science
edited by
Brett Laursen
Florida Atlantic University

MEASUREMENT BURST DESIGNS TO IMPROVE PRECISION IN PEER RESEARCH

Ryan J. Persram
McGill University

Bianca Panarello
Concordia University

Melisa Castellanos
Concordia University

Lisa Astrologo
Concordia University

William M. Bukowski
Concordia University

CAMBRIDGE
UNIVERSITY PRESS

CAMBRIDGE
UNIVERSITY PRESS

University Printing House, Cambridge CB2 8BS, United Kingdom

One Liberty Plaza, 20th Floor, New York, NY 10006, USA

477 Williamstown Road, Port Melbourne, VIC 3207, Australia

314–321, 3rd Floor, Plot 3, Splendor Forum, Jasola District Centre, New Delhi – 110025, India

103 Penang Road, #05–06/07, Visioncrest Commercial, Singapore 238467

Cambridge University Press is part of the University of Cambridge.

It furthers the University's mission by disseminating knowledge in the pursuit of education, learning, and research at the highest international levels of excellence.

www.cambridge.org
Information on this title: www.cambridge.org/9781108986526
DOI: 10.1017/9781108986038

© Ryan J. Persram, Bianca Panarello, Melisa Castellanos, Lisa Astrologo, and William M. Bukowski 2021

First published 2021

A catalogue record for this publication is available from the British Library.

ISBN 978-1-108-98652-6 Paperback
ISSN 2632-9964 (online)
ISSN 2632-9956 (print)

Measurement Burst Designs to Improve Precision in Peer Research

Elements in Research Methods for Developmental Science

DOI: 10.1017/9781108986038
First published online: September 2021

Ryan J. Persram
McGill University

Bianca Panarello
Concordia University

Melisa Castellanos
Concordia University

Lisa Astrologo
Concordia University

William M. Bukowski
Concordia University

Author for correspondence: Ryan J. Persram, ryan.persram@mail.mcgill.ca

Abstract: Measurement burst designs, in which assessments of a set of constructs are made at two or more times in quick succession (e.g., within days), can be used as a novel method to improve the stability of basic measures typically used in longitudinal peer research. In this Element, we hypothesized that the stabilities for adolescent-reported peer acceptance, anxiety, and self-concept would be stronger when using the measurement burst approach versus the single-time observation. Participants included youth between ten and thirteen years old who completed (a) sociometric assessments of acceptance, and measures of (b) social and test anxiety, and (c) self-concept across three times with two assessments made at each burst. Findings broadly showed that the stabilities were significantly stronger with the measurement burst when compared to the single-time assessment, supporting our main hypothesis. We discuss the utility of the measurement burst in a broader context and considerations for researchers.

Keywords: measurement burst, peer research, acceptance, anxiety, self-concept

ISBNs: 9781108986526 (PB), 9781108986038 (OC)
ISSNs: 2632-9964 (online), 2632-9956 (print)

Contents

1 Measurement Burst Designs and Peer Relations

One of the core factors that researchers and practitioners in developmental psychology are concerned with is the concept of change and variability. Longitudinal research methodologies allow scientists and practitioners to investigate how psychological phenomena change or are maintained across a determined period of time. However, in studying change across the lifespan, we must be cognizant of the variability that exists in how and when we measure psychological constructs in general. For example, in the study of internalizing symptoms among children, elevated levels of test anxiety, which refers to the negative internalized feelings experienced when confronted with academically evaluative situations (Spielberger & Vagg, 1995; Sub & Prabha, 2003), might be present due to an upcoming or previously taken exam. Social anxiety differs to test anxiety such that the former is typically associated with negative thoughts prior to, during, or after a social evaluative situation (Hearn et al., 2017), while the latter is more salient to test-taking experiences. Given these differences, levels of test anxiety are not likely to reflect the genuineness of an adolescent's anxious feelings toward tests in general, but rather a time-dependent or "snapshot" moment. One way to address changes and fluctuations in psychological states is via the use of measurement burst designs. With this in mind, we propose that the measurement burst would allow for increasing the accuracy with which we study phenomena common to youth development. Specifically, we focus on peer relationships, a fundamental context that becomes increasingly influential as children become adolescents. In three separate studies, we examine the extent to which the measurement burst design provides more-stable estimates of (1) adolescent experiences with being accepted/liked within the peer group, (2) social and test anxiety, and (3) the general self-concept, which refers to the evaluation of one's own competence to engage, maintain, and experience positive social interactions with others (Harter, 2012).

1.1 Longitudinal Research as Integral to Studying Development

Developmental and quantitative psychologists, including Paul Baltes (1987) and John Nesselroade (1990), have long argued that change and variability at the level of the individual is complex, multidirectional, and multidimensional, hence the need for rigorous measurements. Longitudinal research designs, in which measurements are taken at predetermined points across time, chart the development of the construct or phenomena of interest. These assessments are typically taken only once and then compared with the time points that follow (see Figure 1a). The results, depending on the length of the study, are multiple repeated measures of data points that chart the trajectory or path of a given construct. For example, a study by Eisenberg and colleagues (1999) investigated the development and stability of prosocial dispositions by observing a sample of children from around the age of four or five years until early adulthood. The result was approximately eleven observations across this period of time, which demonstrated that individuals who possessed early prosocial personality dispositions (e.g., engaged in spontaneous sharing in childhood) had higher levels of prosocial behaviours in early adulthood. This widely cited study demonstrates the value of longitudinal research in charting change and variability across multiple developmental periods.

Clearly, longitudinal studies are valuable in demonstrating the degree to which change and variability occur. However, there are four main limitations to note. First, conducting longitudinal research can be financially costly and labour-intensive. Expenses directed to recruitment, maintenance, and completion of a study can contribute to increased costs with designing a longitudinal study. Second, as with other research designs, the risk of participant attrition and burnout is high. A study as intensive as that of Eisenberg et al. (1999) originally consisted of thirty-seven children but obtained a final sample size of thirty-two. The loss of five participants may not seem like a significant one, but it can be particularly harmful for longitudinal research in which participants are asked to be involved for months or even years. Similarly, a meta-analysis assessing the effects of cognitive behaviour therapy on chronic pain found that attrition rates in samples of children can range from 0 to 54 percent (Karlson & Rapoff, 2009). The cost-benefit of being involved for so long, coupled with trying to take advantage of the longitudinal design in order to measure a number of different constructs, can increase participant burnout, consequently increasing the likelihood of attrition. As a result, high attrition rates can have detrimental consequences for the generalizability of a study's findings (e.g., Gustavson et al., 2012). Regardless, the information obtained from longitudinal research plays a fundamental role in developmental research; consequently, methods to prevent participant burnout and attrition should be valued in our research.

The third limitation reflects on the measurement process more broadly. Whereas the Eisenberg et al. (1999) study was able to use multiple annual time points to measure prosocial dispositions, other studies have shorter time frames to work with, resulting in fewer observations. For example, a longitudinal study of video gaming assessed children and adolescents across three time points and observed that greater amounts of video gaming, among other factors, were risk factors for becoming pathological gamers (Gentile et al., 2011). The difference between these studies reflects an important limitation, in that having so few measurements, namely one at each time, can be influenced by other circumstances that occur at that given time. For example, the time at which video-gaming frequency was measured could be influenced by the fact that children had less work to do at that specific time. Relatedly, when developmental researchers measure self-concept among youth, an adolescent's self-reported high score on a single-time assessment of their positive self-concept might be inflated because they received compliments on their appearance or performed extremely well on a test. Thus, that positive self-concept at the level of the adolescent may not be indicative of their true sense of self or what they feel. As such, it can be argued that while longitudinal designs can be useful for assessing changes in trait values, they do not allow researchers the opportunity to capture "systematic time- or situation-specific 'ups and downs' in individual's true state scores around the fixed trait" (Geiser et al., 2015, p. 2).

The fourth limitation reflects participant burden. Individuals who conduct research with humans and other animals face multiple challenges. One challenge is project completion. After assembling the needed funds, one needs to put the plans for the study into action. The basic criteria for success include having a sufficiently large sample that is representative of the target population and having a minimal amount or proportion of missing data. A further criterion for a longitudinal study is maintaining sample membership across the times of assessment. A second challenge concerns data quality. Our measures need to reach well-known psychometric standards of validity and reliability. To reach these stringent expectations, we need to use measures and procedures that will produce well-focused measures and that minimize measurement error. A third challenge concerns the ethical commitments researchers make to the participants in our studies and to the contexts where their projects occur. Researchers make a promise to the participants in their studies that their participation will not be a source of stress greater than what is "normal" in their daily lives. They also make a commitment, either explicitly or implicitly, to minimize the intrusive disruptions they bring to the contexts where their studies take place. These ethical commitments are a basic duty of research scientists.

These four challenges are situated in different domains. The first has to do with procedural issues related to obtaining and maintaining a proper sample. The second concerns the adequacy of measurements. The third is about ethics. Despite the differences between these challenges, each of them is linked to a critical but often overlooked concept known as participant or respondent burden. Participant burden refers to the demands placed on individuals who take part in a research study (Sharp & Frankel, 1983). This concept is not new. Discussions of it have been seen in the health and social science literatures for 100 years (Chapin, 1920). We conceptualize participant burden as having a curvilinear rather than a linear association with time.

Due to this time-related exponential increase in participant burden, the increased burden of a twenty-minute assessment period compared with a fifteen-minute period will be smaller than an increase from twenty minutes to twenty-five minutes when studying other constructs.

Participant burden has ethical and pragmatic consequences (Lingler et al., 2014). The ethical consequences are related to our commitment that participation in our studies will not be a source of stress. When participant burden is high, we violate this commitment. This violation occurs at the level of the individual participant and at the level of the contexts where we conduct our studies. At both levels, we do not live up to our agreement to treat research participants in an ethical manner. The pragmatic consequences of participant burden have to do with the quality of the data that are collected and with the continuity in participation in longitudinal studies. To the degree that participant burden causes fatigue and distraction, it will undermine a participant's motivation and ability to provide honest and accurate answers. These conditions will decrease the reliability and validity of our data. Reduced validity and reliability have an adverse effect on the adequacy of our studies. Another negative consequence is increased levels of attrition. Participants who feel burdened by their initial experiences in a study are unlikely to continue. Given that this form of attrition is not likely to be random, it will decrease the representativeness of a sample. It will also decrease the size of the sample. Both of these effects reduce the value of our studies. That being said, we recognize that true measurement burst designs can increase participant burden, depending on the intensity of the assessment, such as having participants provide emotional state ratings multiple times per day for thirty days. However, it can also help to ease the burden when it is incorporated as part of larger studies. Here, we posit that a measurement burst design can contribute by minimizing participant burden. Our point is that having two or more abbreviated assessment sessions instead of one very long session will reduce the demands we place on our participants and, as a consequence, will improve the ethical standards of our projects and will increase the quality of our data. In the following sections, we demonstrate how participant burden is reduced by having two testing sessions within each burst, which lasts between thirty and forty-five minutes. This would be in contrast to having a single session that lasts between sixty and ninety minutes, which is problematic. For example, having such long sessions significantly reduces class time for teachers and can increase the cognitive load imposed on students to focus on questionnaires that researchers ask them to take seriously. As such, multiple sessions that are shorter in length help to ease these burdens.

1.2 Measurement Burst Design Methodology

The measurement burst design methodology is an intensive form of assessment in which two or more measures are made in quick succession within time points, otherwise known as a burst (Sliwinski, 2008). Specifically, it provides a means of detecting *intraindividual* variability and change in one's mood and related emotions and behaviours by using multiple short-term measurements in a longitudinal research design (Nesselroade, 1990; Sliwinski, 2008). For example, in a three-wave longitudinal study that measures the stability of anxiety across the school year, each burst would consist of two (at minimum) assessments or observations, separated by one week, resulting in six observations for each participant (see Figure 1b). When multiple observations are taken within the same time point, we can increase the precision with which we are measuring the phenomena of interest by considering momentary deviations in state mood levels that can occur from one time point to the next as a result of external factors beyond the control of the researcher. In doing so, the high degree of measurement overlap within burst designs should produce a more stable estimate across time because of the increased accuracy of the two measures of the same construct. Specifically, a measurement burst design helps researchers understand nuanced changes in an individual's self-reported state at different points in time.

Sliwinski (2008, 2011) describes measurement burst designs as a way of capturing two extreme forms of longitudinal research designs. Indeed, the measurement burst design is a mix between longitudinal designs in which there are more widely spaced intervals and those in which data are collected in quick succession (e.g., daily diaries, experience sampling methods/ecological momentary assessments). The former captures more broad changes obtained at one point in time, while the latter allows for more fine-grained analyses of phenomena that may be prone to increased variability, such as affective states and self-esteem (e.g., Nelis & Bukowski, 2019). Importantly, the measurement burst design can help to disentangle whether the differences observed across bursts are typical ups and downs in one's mood versus an enduring change in one's trait mood over time (Geiser et al., 2015). As such, the measurement burst design offers a wide array of advantages over and above the two extremes of longitudinal data collection, including improved measurement of various phenomena (Stawski et al., 2016). For example, measurement burst designs allow for multiple, intensive measurements that increase the precision of the construct (e.g., anxiety) but also the reliability of the instrument being used. In addition, they also afford researchers the opportunity to maximize the data collection process by collecting as much information as possible while reducing

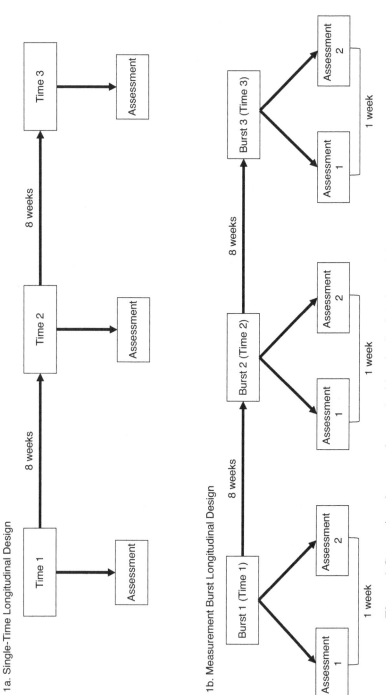

Figure 1 Comparison between the standard longitudinal design and the measurement burst design

participant burden and fatigue. Moreover, measurement bursts allow researchers to study the dynamics of change over multiple time points, namely within the bursts and over a longer time period, which is the overarching goal of developmental science (Sliwinski, 2008; Stawski et al., 2016).

The general approach of a measurement burst design study involves three main steps, two of which involve deciding on the temporal sampling of data within and across time points. Rast and colleagues (2012) argue that different patterns of variability emerge as a function of the construct under study. Typically, the longitudinal aspect ranges in months or even years. In our studies, we used three time points (known as bursts) within an academic school year. Time 1 (T1) was shortly after the beginning of the school year. Time 2 (T2) occurred approximately eight weeks later, which was followed by Time 3 (T3) that took place around eight weeks after T2. These time points were chosen to reflect the uncertainty that typically comes with entering a new grade at the beginning of the school year and at two points in which they should, in theory, be more comfortable with and knowledgeable about their class. The second step was to decide how often to collect data (i.e., assessments within bursts). Although there does not appear to be a set of rules that dictate how many and how often assessments within bursts should be conducted, there should be multiple assessments done in quick succession. This would suggest that the interval between assessments be short, such as days or a week. Another consideration to be made is the time investment on the part of the participants as well as other stakeholders. The goal of researchers should be to make the best use of the time participants take to give high-quality responses, and to do so by minimizing burden. In our studies, we had to consider the time allotted to us in the classroom. In this case, to minimize participant burden and maximize the valuable time afforded to us by teachers, each burst had two assessments, one week apart. The third step involves the methodological approach. In their chapter, Cho and colleagues (2019) highlight studies that demonstrate the utility of measurement bursts using various approaches, including daily diary data (e.g., Almeida et al., 2009) and ecological momentary assessments (EMAs) whose range can vary between minutes, hours, and days (e.g., Liao et al., 2017), and combinations of both (e.g., Scott et al., 2015). Each assessment type evaluates an individual's self-reported state and experience, which can then be used to chart change and variability.

A review of studies that apply measurement burst designs shows that they are often used with adult populations, studying change and variability in the physical, cognitive, and social-emotional domains (e.g., Lee et al., 2018; Scott et al., 2015; Sliwinski et al., 2010). However, there is evidence for its use with younger samples as well (see Riediger & Rauers, 2018 for a review of experience sampling in developmental research). For example, a daily diary study examined the effects of students' trait self-regulation and perceived task difficulty on task enjoyment and independence from their parents during home-schooling as a result of the COVID-19 pandemic (Blume et al., 2020). Parents reported on their children's learning independence, perception of task difficulty, and enjoyment once a day for twenty-two days. There were three main findings to note on the within-person and between-person levels. First, there were positive associations between trait self-regulation and learning independence. Second, learning independence was found to be higher on days when tasks were seen as being easier, whereas on days in which tasks were difficult, learning independence was lower. Third, higher average task enjoyment was associated with greater learning independence, suggesting that those who enjoyed their task were also more independent than those who did not enjoy it. Studies such as the one by Blume and colleagues support the utility of measurement burst designs within the context of child development and functioning.

To our knowledge, the use of measurement burst designs is still emerging in peer research. Whereas cross-sectional intensive measurement designs are not new, incorporating them into longitudinal measurement burst designs is indeed novel. For example, a study by Lehman and Repetti (2007) explored the effects of negative school (e.g., academic problems) events on children's functioning using daily reports across five days. Their results showed that on days when youth reported greater problems in the academic or peer domain during the school day, they were more likely to report aversive interactions with their parents, suggesting that peer experiences contribute to variability in children's functioning. More recent work by Schmidt and colleagues (2020) examined associations between relatedness satisfaction and relatedness frustration at school on child-reported positive and negative affect. Participants reported on these measures twice daily for two weeks (Study 1) and then once a day for four weeks (Studies 2 and 3). Broadly, their findings showed positive associations between relatedness satisfaction and positive affect, and between relatedness frustration and negative affect at the between-person level. Moreover, relatedness frustration positively predicted negative affect, suggesting that variations in children's reports of having less-than-positive encounters with peers were associated with greater negative affect. They also showed within-person level findings on the positive effect of relatedness satisfaction on positive affect, indicating that children who had positive interactions with their peers demonstrated more positive affect. Though cross-sectionally designed, these studies represent initial attempts to incorporate measurement bursts into peer research, which indeed support its utility, despite requiring further investigations.

Given the degree of change and stability in various facets of a child's or an adolescent's life, the measurement burst design nested within longitudinal research can help to increase the reliability of the measures being evaluated. With this in mind, this Element aims to provide evidence for the application of burst designs within the domain of peer relations research among early adolescents in three different ways. In particular, our goal is to demonstrate that measurement bursts offer more-accurate estimates than single-time estimates on constructs commonly studied in peer research. In Section 2, we demonstrate the effects of the burst in sociometric ratings and nominations of acceptance, which are fundamental measures within peer research. In Sections 3 and 4, we focus on self-reports of core psychological concepts related to early adolescent experiences with internalizing problems (i.e., social and test anxiety) and the self-concept (or self-worth). In these sections, we hypothesize that the stability between the respective measures will be stronger when the burst model is applied, in comparison to typical longitudinal designs in which one assessment is made at each time point.

1.3 Peer Relations as a Developmental Context

Social relationships are part of the fabric of the human experience. The relationships individuals have with others can significantly impact the well-being and overall functioning of everyone involved. Peer relationships are commonly seen as a particularly salient context through which youth development can be studied. Research on peer relations in childhood and adolescence extends to the early days of experimental psychology (Bukowski et al., 2018; Monroe, 1898). The interactions that youth have with their peers represent some of the crucial social relationships that play a role in one's well-being and development. Unlike family relationships, peer relations are unique in that they are voluntary and are more balanced in terms of power (e.g., Howe et al., 2011; Laursen & Bukowski, 1997). As such, peers offer a unique insight into how extrafamilial relationships can affect the developmental trajectories of children and adolescents.

Many studies within the peer domain tend to use the longitudinal design framework to examine various correlates and consequences associated with peer relations. For example, the *Child Development Project* is a longitudinal data set that began when children were five years old and followed them through adolescence, which includes approximately nine waves of measurement (see Dodge et al., 1990; Pettit et al., 2001). Findings using this data set have shown several different results related to peers. Specifically, Criss et al. (2002) found that grade 1 children's level of peer acceptance moderated the positive association between experiences with externalizing behaviours in the second grade, suggesting that positive peer experiences could be protective against individual stressors. Another data set, known as the *Waterloo Longitudinal Project* (see

Hymel et al., 1990), investigated youth development within the peer context using school-age children beginning at around five years old. In this case, Rubin and colleagues (1990) found social withdrawal to be stable during early school years and that it was positively associated with depression, feelings of loneliness, and negative self-perceptions of competence in late childhood. These findings tend to remain consistent across many studies on peer experiences; namely, those who experience greater peer rejection at one time show greater levels of externalizing (Hymel et al., 1990) and internalizing problems (Prinstein et al., 2005), at least three years after the initial data collection. Taken together, the enduring nature of peer research has allowed for the study of youth development from childhood to adolescence and has provided unique insights into the role of peers. However, as important as these longitudinal designs are to understanding change and variability in the peer context, the single-measurement approach has limited our ability to fully establish accuracy in what we are measuring within and across time.

Peer research often includes a variety of ways in which indices of acceptance, rejection, and individual well-being are measured. Two of the most common methods used among adolescents include sociometric assessments and self-reports. Sociometric assessments are the standard method of studying one's experience with peers (Bukowski et al., 2017; Cillessen & Bukowski, 2018). Typically, acceptance and liking within the peer group is measured via nominations of a participant's limited or unlimited choice of rank-ordered "same-sex" and "other-sex" friends (Bukowski & Newcomb, 1984; Coie et al., 1982; Newcomb & Bukowski, 1983). A follow-up assessment then asks participants to rate how much they like their classmates on a five-point Likert scale ranging from 1 ("not at all") to 5 ("like very much"). From there, nomination scores and liking ratings are produced, accounting for various factors including class size. Currently, there are multiple recent and comprehensive manuscripts that describe these procedures in detail, including a special issue by Marks (2017), as well as manuscripts by Bukowski et al., (2017), Cillessen and Bukowski (2018), and Velásquez et al. (2013). Clearly, sociometric assessments are the most broadly used method for evaluating how liked and accepted children and adolescents are within their peer group.

The second common method is through self-reported assessments of well-being and functioning. This is especially the case for adolescents, who are more capable than younger children of precisely describing their feelings, experiences, and thoughts on a variety of constructs, including anxiety (Wood et al., 2017), friendship (Persram et al., 2021), and self-concept (Nelis & Bukowski, 2019). By adolescence, cognitive gains generally include the ability to engage in self-evaluations and social comparisons with one's peers. Given this skill, adolescent participants are able to provide researchers with ratings that they feel represent them best. Their ratings can also benefit from other formats of collecting data, as they can be evaluated for concordance. For example, when participants are asked via peer assessment to nominate someone in their class "Who is anxious …, " those nominations can be used in tandem with self-reports of anxiety to identify how these measures correspond with each other and to assess how accurately the class and the participant view their levels of anxiety.

Regardless of how adolescents respond to their peer experiences, each instrument should have strong psychometric properties. In the case of self-reported data, measures of reliability such as Cronbach's alpha (α) (Cronbach, 1951) or the omega coefficient (ω) (MacDonald, 1999) provide evidence for the degree to which items are internally consistent and broadly reflect the construct of interest. In the case of sociometric assessments, however, reliability is not easily calculated because it consists of a single item. Despite this, it has become generally accepted across the peer literature that a single item that taps into peer acceptance is reliable because of its use of multiple informants (Bukowski et al., 2012). Specifically, each participant in a given researcher-defined reference group (e.g., classroom) responds to the same set of single items such as "How much do you like …" and "Who are three best friends" for every person in that class, resulting in given *and* received scores for nominations and ratings. Since all participants in that given class or reference group respond to that item with the same response options as in a self-reported Likert-scale item, we can infer that this is a reliable approach to studying peer acceptance. That said, as reliable and valid as self-reports and sociometric assessments can be, they are still open to variability because of circumstances beyond a researcher's control. For example, experiences within the peer group can vary depending on the day as a result of positive or negative experiences; hence, youth may adjust who they like or who are their top friends, as reported by Lehman and Repetti (2007). Just as in the early example of finding a student's potentially exaggerated levels of test anxiety over an upcoming test, a measurement burst design would clarify whether this student's high levels of test anxiety are stable or a result of a particular experience occurring close to data collection. In doing so, researchers would benefit from having more data points to chart developmental changes but also have increased confidence in the data they have obtained.

Typically, reliability is estimated using the alpha coefficient, which assesses the degree to which items within a given scale are internally consistent. It generally follows a classical test theory's notion that there is one measurement error (Geldhof et al., 2014). Alpha considers the covariance of the items within a given scale, the variance of the total scale score, as well as the number of items included in the scale in its estimate. Thus, higher alpha estimates suggest greater consistency between items, leading researchers to argue that each of the items are correlated high enough and cluster together as a scale. There are a number of drawbacks, however, to the use of alpha. One such limitation is that as the number of items on a measure increases, alpha is also likely to increase (Carmines & Zeller, 1979; Nezlek, 2017). Relatedly, once alpha has reached an acceptable threshold to be considered *internally consistent*, which ideally is greater than .75, there is little to be gained by seeking to improve it. Moreover, since alpha does assume one type of measurement error, it does not factor the hierarchical structure of the data, making it possible for estimates to be biased (Geldhof et al., 2014). Alpha is the preferred index when items in a given scale measure the same construct and are obtained during one assessment (Taber et al., 2018) and when aggregated scores are created by computing an arithmetic mean of a set of ratings while giving equal weight to each rating alpha. Conversely, omega is the preferred index if the ratings are to be combined by weighting items according to the factor loadings observed in an exploratory or confirmatory analysis.

In order to overcome such issues, peer research would benefit from employing multilevel confirmatory factor analyses (MCFA) (see Geldhof et al., 2014; Rush & Hofer, 2017 for reviews), which use the factor loadings to determine the true score variance to total variance ratio. Geldhof and colleagues (2014) argue that while the MCFA align more with the generalizability theoretical approach, in which a scale for a given construct's total variance can be broken into a number of unique factors (e.g., variance of a person's deviation from a grand mean, variance of specific items), these values can be interpreted as reliability estimates. The MCFA provides two ω estimates: (1) within-person and (2) between-person multilevel estimates, where higher estimates suggest greater reliability or consistency. The within-person ω coefficient is the ratio of true within-person variance to total within-person variance and is the covariance between each of the items on each occasion or assessment. The between-person ω is the ratio of true between-person variance relative to the total between-person variance and is the covariance between items that is aggregated over time (Geldhof et al., 2017). Compared to the within-person estimate, the between-person estimate is often higher (Rush & Hofer, 2017). In the following studies, the multilevel ω estimate treats the items (defined as Level 1) nested within occasion or day of assessment (defined as Level 2). We compare these estimates to demonstrate the increased preciseness, which accounts for the nested structure of the data.

1.4 The Goal of this Element

To our knowledge, burst designs have not been explicitly used within the peer context. As such, the objective of this Element is to provide empirical support for the claim that measurement burst designs have a high degree of utility in the study of peer relations. Given the wide-ranging influence of peer relationships, our aim is to demonstrate that collecting data using short bursts within a longitudinal research design can provide researchers with more precise and reliable measurements on constructs prone to vary as a result of day-to-day experiences, and an individual's perception at a very specific moment in time. Specifically, we have identified three commonly studied experiences that youth have with their peers that would be amenable to the use of measurement bursts. These include the degree to which they are accepted/liked by their peers (Section 2), their feelings of anxiety in social and test situations (Section 3), and their perceptions of the self (Section 4). In these studies, we predict that the burst design approach will produce stronger, more reliable estimates of peer acceptance, anxiety, and social concept over time when compared with measures taken at either the first or second burst.

1.5 General Method and Plan of Analysis

In each of the following three sections, we tested the stabilities of the respective constructs using a three-wave measurement burst design in multiple datasets. The design for each of the datasets was similar in that they occurred over the course of a given school year. As we previously alluded to, Time 1 (T1) was typically at or just after the beginning of the school year, Time 2 (T2) occurred approximately eight weeks later, and Time 3 (T3) followed eight weeks after T2. Within each burst two assessments were collected within one week of each other. As such, six observations were made for each participant. In each section they will be denoted as Burst 1 Assessment 1 (T1-1), Burst 1 Assessment 2, (T1-2), Burst 2 Assessment 1 (T2-1), Burst 2 Assessment 2 (T2-2), Burst 3 Assessment 1 (T3-1), and Burst 3, Assessment 2 (T3-2). Data were collected using INQUISIT software, which is an electronic survey administration tool for collecting psychological measurements. Measures included sociometric assessments of the peer group within each of the classrooms and self-report measures of anxiety and the self-concept. The specific measures used will be described in greater detail in their respective sections.

1.5.1 Participants

Three separate but similar samples of participants were used across the three sections in this Element and consisted of a broad representation of socioeconomic status. Participants were early adolescents in grades 5 and 6 from Montréal, Canada and Barranquilla, Colombia (Sample 2). The samples we report were part of a larger study, but we focus on the measures of peer acceptance, anxiety, and self-concept findings as they were studied with the measurement burst approach.

Sample 1. Sample 1 consisted of 394 adolescents from 22 classrooms in fifth and sixth grade between the ages of 10 and 12 years (51% male) from four mixed-gender primary schools in Montréal, Canada. On average, the participation rate per classroom was high ($M = 83\%$, range = 64–100%). In Canada, SES was based on information provided by the school as well as census data regarding education and median income. Among the four schools to participate in this study, two were designated as upper-middle class ($n = 231$) and the other two were classified as lower-middle class ($n = 163$).

Sample 2. Sample 2 consisted of 351 fifth and sixth grade students, between 10 and 12 years old (168 male, 183 female), from Barranquilla, Colombia ($N = 174$) and Montréal, Canada ($N = 177$). Data were collected from 11 separate classrooms from five mixed-gender schools in lower-middle and upper-middle class neighbourhoods. Three schools from Montréal participated in this study, one of which was designated as upper-middle class ($n = 79$) and the other two as lower-middle class ($n = 98$). In Colombia, the designation for these classes is based on the government-assigned *estrato* index, ranging from 1 to 6, with higher scores indicating neighbourhoods with greater affluence. There were two schools that participated in this study, one of which was upper-middle (estrato 5 to 6) ($n = 74$), while the other school was designated as lower-middle (estrato 2 to 3) ($n = 100$). The participation rate per classroom was high ($M = 89\%$, range = 75–100%).

Sample 3. Sample 3 consisted of 164 fifth and sixth grade students between 10 and 12 years old (87 male, 77 female) attending two schools in Montréal, Canada. There were 11 classrooms that represented 80% of the potential pool of participants (range = 70–94%). The mean age of the participants was 11.5 years. In this study, one school was designated as lower-middle class ($n = 67$), while the other was classified as upper-middle class ($n = 97$).

1.5.2 Procedure

The procedure of the studies whose findings we report in this Element was approved by the Human Research Ethics Committee at Concordia University. The title of our application was One World / Whole Child (approval number: 3000279). We also obtained informed consent from the school board and the school principals. In each of the three samples, adolescents were recruited in their classrooms during class time and were provided with detailed letters outlining the objectives and requirements of the current study to bring home to their primary caregiver. Child assent was obtained, and parental consent forms were signed and returned to each child's classroom teacher. Adolescents that did not return a signed consent letter or rescinded their assent were not included in the data analyses. Once parental consent was obtained and the classroom recruitment phase was completed, the dates during which the three waves of data collection (T1, T2, and T3) would take place were arranged with each participating school. Participating children completed self-report questionnaires at their desks during class time using tablet computers at six separate times across the school year. Trained members of the research team were present during each data collection. If at any point a child wished to discontinue their participation, their data was discarded. There were no specific inclusion/exclusion criteria across all samples. For all Spanish-speaking participants in Sample 2, consent forms, documents, and items were all translated and back-translated by native Spanish speakers who were also fluent in English to ensure proper translation and Spanish dialect (see Appendix for all items and anchors).

1.5.3 Plan of Analysis

Analyses for each of these sections will follow the same three general steps. First, in line with data management in peer research, all missing data were dealt with via multiple imputation performed with Mplus (Ver. 6.0; Muthén & Muthén, 2010). Second, with the exception of the section on sociometric assessments, internal consistency was calculated using two types of reliability indices. The first is Cronbach's alpha, which was computed for (1) each assessment (i.e., single-time assessment) and (2) across each burst, which were the items across both assessments. The second is a two-level multilevel omega estimate which provides within- and between-level indices of reliability (see Geldhof et al., 2014). Third, across-time Pearson bivariate correlations were estimated which compare the variables within each of the two assessments across the three times (i.e., T1-1 with T2-1, T1-2 with T2-2, T2-1 with T3-1, T2-2 with T3-2) with additional correlations between each time (T1 with T2 and T2 with T3). To do so, two sets of scores were computed. First, single-time estimates were calculated, which was an average of the items within each assessment (e.g., mean of positive general self-concept at T1-1) and provide a participant's average score on a given measure at that particular time. The second score was an average of those same items at each time (e.g., mean of social anxiety items at T1-1 and T1-2) and provides an average response across both assessments that make up that given time. For each correlation, the 95% confidence interval was computed using the Fisher's z-transformation (Bonnet & Wright, 2000). The general approach can be seen in Figure 1, where we compared the single-time longitudinal design (Figure 1a) with the measurement burst design (Figure 1b). These comparisons were conducted using Steiger's (1980) calculations to test for the difference between dependent correlations.

Steiger's (1980) statistical approach allows for a comparison across a correlation matrix. In other words, this approach is a useful tool that allows for statistical comparisons across correlation coefficients measured on the same individual and across constructs that are related. In our analyses, the item(s) in Burst 1 are also found in the same constructs being compared in Burst 2. Thus, the correlations being compared are expected to be highly correlated at the start, given that we are comparing scores across the same individuals and across items that pertain to constructs being compared across each burst. The analyses based on Steiger's (1980) approach allow for the comparisons of two correlations while controlling for the shared variance across both correlations. Here, differences are reflected as z-scores, in which scores more extreme than an absolute value of 1.96 (assuming an alpha of .05) are observed to be statistically significant.

Although our primary goal is to provide empirical evidence to support the use of measurement burst designs in peer research, we also argue that this approach is much needed in a broader context. Our aim is to show that burst designs can be used to increase our precision in studying change in adolescent development, broadly construed. It is evident that psychological and social constructs change and vary at different rates. Thus, measurement bursts can account for this to provide more accurate estimates at the rate and pace that these changes occur. As such, developmental research, especially in childhood and adolescence, would greatly benefit from having more data points within each burst of assessment in order to assess how much change does occur at each point.

2 Sociometric Assessments of Peer Acceptance

After nearly a century, the study of peer influence continues to be a fundamental focal point for developmental researchers. Human interactions play a vital role in development (Hinde, 1979; Laursen & Bukowski, 1997). This is particularly relevant in adolescence, a time in development that is exceptionally sensitive to the mechanisms of fostering and maintaining interpersonal relationships with peers (Brown & Larson, 2009). The use of sociometric assessments, which refers to the method of assessing social relationships within the context of a peer group, is considered the gold standard for developmental researchers who explore the domain of peer relations (Bukowski et al., 2017). At the outset, the main purpose of sociometric assessments was to identify children who were accepted (i.e., how well-liked they are) and rejected (i.e., how disliked they are) by their peers with the goal of identifying those that were in problematic peer relationships (Cillessen & Bukowski, 2018). This was done by asking participants within a reference group (e.g., a classroom) to identify the peers that they "liked the most" and "liked the least" in order to classify a participant's standing within that reference group (Coie et al, 1982; Newcomb & Bukowski, 1983). Regardless of its widespread use, the psychometric properties of sociometric assessments are examined rarely (cf. Bukowski & Newcomb, 1983). Since the 1950s, few studies have examined the reliability and validity of sociometric assessments. A major exception to this practice is the assessment of one-month test rest reliability of measures of acceptance and rejection in a sample of preadolescent girls and boys (Bukowski & Newcomb, 1984). This assessment was conducted twice, once just before and once just after the participants transitioned from an elementary-school to a middle-school environment. Across these one-month time periods, the cross-time correlation for the measure of acceptance was .76 for the one-month period prior to the transition and .74 for the one-month period after the transition. If the two scores from each of these one-month periods were combined to create a single score for each period, the observed reliabilities (i.e., alpha) would be .86 and .85 for the pre-transition and the post-transition scores, respectively. Corresponding values for a measure of rejection were the correlations of .78 and .65 and reliability measures of .88 and .79. It should be noted that this study from thirty-seven years ago used a burst design format. Evidence from this study supports the view that sociometric measures are reliable. The field of sociometric assessment has continuously evolved and been refined using contemporary statistical and measurement methods; however, the psychometric properties of a tool that is so often used could be better understood. Accordingly, the purpose of this section is to test a statistical approach that we argue could improve the reliability of sociometric assessment scores across time in an adolescent sample. Specifically, the goal of this section is to demonstrate that a measurement burst design consisting of three bursts (two assessments per burst) versus a single time of data collection will provide more stable and reliable measures of sociometric assessment scores.

2.1 Sociometric Assessment

The study of peer relations is multifaceted, as the peer context can be analyzed at the level of the individual, the dyad, and the group when using sociometric assessments (Rubin, Bukowski, & Bowker, 2006). Sociometric assessments can be conducted with either nominations or ratings (Asher & Dodge, 1986; Bukowski & Hoza, 1989; Bukowski et al., 2017). With a nomination technique, children indicate which of their peers are their friends. An acceptance score is calculated for each child, indicating how often the child was chosen as a friend by peers. With a rating scale measure, every child rates how much they like each of their participating peers on a scale whose lowest value, typically a 1, means "do not like," and whose highest value, typically a 5, means "like very much." Using these ratings, an acceptance score is calculated for each child, indicating how often the child received the highest rating from peers. It has been shown already that rating and nomination measures of acceptance can be scale combined to create a reliable aggregated measure (Asher & Dodge, 1985; Bukowski et al. 2000).

2.2 The Developmental Significance of Peer Groups

The peer context in childhood and adolescence is often characterized as being complex and multidimensional. It is amongst peers where adolescents create voluntary relationships that are novel in their levels of intimacy (e.g., romantic partners, intimate friendships; Brown & Larson, 2009; Laursen & Bukowski, 1997), which offers unique opportunities to foster skills such as interpersonal social proficiency and methods of cooperation (Parker et al., 2006). Extant research on peer relations often aims to categorize their sample by determining who are sociometrically accepted (i.e., liked by many, disliked by few) and sociometrically rejected (i.e., liked by few, disliked by many) within the reference group (LaFontana & Cillessen, 2010). Moreover, while there is a general consensus across developmental researchers that the peer context aids youth in developing their sense of self, peer relations can also have long-term consequences on well-being that can be both beneficial and harmful across the lifespan (Parker et al., 2006). Specifically, accepted adolescents are usually described as being prosocial and tend to maintain higher school achievement than less-liked peers (McDonald & Asher, 2018; Newcomb et al., 1993). Conversely, having low levels of classroom acceptance and friendship quality was found to be associated with higher levels of teacher-reported maladjustment within the context of a classroom (Waldrip et al., 2008). Similarly, peer rejection could lead a child to endorse negative and/or distorted social cognitions, and emotion regulation difficulties (Cillessen & Borch, 2006; Zimmer-Gembeck, 2016). Moreover, less-liked adolescents are more likely to experience peer victimization, whereas being well liked by one's reference group appears to mitigate the negative consequences of being disliked by others (de Bruyn et al., 2010; Zimmer-Gembeck, 2016). Specifically, having positive friendships with peers appears to mitigate the negative consequences of not being well liked within a reference group for youth (Waldrip, et al., 2008). In particular, well-liked adolescents are known to maintain more flexible levels of social-cognitive behavioural abilities, such that they are more prosocial, cooperative, fluent in social perspective taking, and have a higher emotional intelligence, which contribute to the useful skill of being able to more accurately perceive both oneself and others in social situations (de Bruyn et al., 2010; Cillessen, 2008). While acceptance is well understood to have an impact on youth's ability to adjust within their context, the opposite association is also known to be true. Maladjustment within a social peer context is associated with negative consequences on well-being (e.g., self-esteem, Kingery, Erdley, & Marshall, 2011). Put another way, the association between the constructs of acceptance and adjustment in adolescents is bidirectional in nature and associated with various factors relating to well-being. Thus, understanding and managing the expectations and opinions of peers becomes increasingly important as a child transitions into adolescence (Brown & Larson, 2009; Laursen & Bukowski, 1997). This has implications on the relevance and importance placed on the peer context within the realm of development.

2.3 The Developmental Trajectory of Acceptance

Existing research that examines the developmental trajectory of acceptance in adolescence typically does so in tandem with other social behaviours (e.g., aggression, popularity) while utilizing single-time data collections. Important to note is the distinction between acceptance and popularity. While acceptance is a measure of how well-liked a child is within their peer group, popularity refers to an individual's social prestige, social power, and/or social visibility within the peer group (Cillessen & van den Berg, 2012; Cillessen et al., 2011). The overlap between popularity and acceptance exists mostly in childhood and decreases exponentially in early adolescence (Cillessen & Borch, 2006; Cillessen & Mayeux, 2004). Thus, although popularity and acceptance are interrelated across development, it has been well established that they are distinct constructs (Parkhurst & Hopmeyer, 1998). For the purpose of this section, we will focus on the sociometric ratings and nominations of peer acceptance.

Moreover, acceptance has a linear and relatively stable trajectory across development (Cillessen & Borch, 2006; Terry & Coie, 1991). Many longitudinal studies, typically utilizing single data collection methods, have demonstrated the stability of peer acceptance scores across time (Jiang & Cillessen, 2005; Terry & Coie, 1991; Tomada & Schneider, 1997). Moreover, a meta-analytic review consisting of seventy-seven studies including over 18,000 children and adolescents (age range 3.5–16 years) further demonstrated the adequate stability of sociometric assessments of peer acceptance across short-term (less than three months) and long-term (greater than three months) longitudinal studies (Jiang & Cillessen, 2005). Yet, Jiang and Cillessen (2005) found two factors that influence the stability of socio-metric assessments of peer acceptance: age and interval length of the study. Specifically, an interaction effect was found for both age and interval length of the study, such that as age and interval length increased, stability of peer acceptance scores decreased. We posit that the use of a burst methodology could potentially minimize the variance created by longer testing intervals within longitudinal methodologies.

2.4 Assessing Sociometric Measures

Clearly, the peer context offers a unique form of measurement for behaviours that are not easily observable such as affect toward an individual (Cillessen & Marks, 2017). Moreover, sociometric assessment offers a distinctive insight into a context that is not easily penetrated from external observation. A meta-analysis consisting of seventy-four studies found a low to moderate cross-informant concordance regarding a measure of social competence across primary caregivers, teachers, and the self-reports of children and adolescents (Renk & Phares, 2004). Since every informant reporting on a child or adolescent's behaviour knows them from different perspectives and contexts, peer relations research offers a unique perspec-tive of how the adolescent is viewed by peers, which may vary from perceptions teachers and primary caregivers may have regarding the adolescent. Furthermore, peers tend to spend more time together, particularly within the school context (Cillessen & Marks, 2017). Yet, it is often questioned whether single-item measure-ments that are typically employed by sociometric assessments are reliable to assess social standing within a reference group (Cillessen & Marks, 2017). While some note that the psychometric properties of sociometric assessment may seem unusual and have not been widely studied, general consensus has been reached in the field that this is a valid and reliable measure of peer relations, given the nature of data collection (Cillessen & Marks, 2017; Lindzey & Borgatta, 1954). Specifically, researchers argue that while there may not be multiple items assessing a particular construct, multiple informants (i.e., the entire reference group) are each providing information for that single item (Cillessen & Marks, 2017). Thus, the peer context affords researchers a different and valid perspective of social behaviours within a particular reference group.

2.5 Goals of This Section

The main purpose of this section is to determine whether a burst design methodology could provide more accurate and stable measurement of acceptance within an adolescent age group. Accordingly, the stability of the acceptance scores from the burst measurement design across three times and the single time measure will be compared. We hypothesize that using a measurement burst design will provide a more stable assessment of this construct compared to a single-time measurement design. Specifically, we expect the stability coefficient for the single time measure to be significantly smaller than the one for the measurement burst design.

2.6 Method

2.6.1 Participants

To determine its replicability, we used two datasets that employed the burst design format to assess peer acceptance. In this section, participants from Sample 1 ($N = 394$) and Sample 2 ($N = 351$) (described earlier) were included in the analyses.

2.6.2 Measures

Participants from both samples completed sociometric assessments at each of the six assessment times (T1-1, T1-2, T2-1, T2-2, T3-1, and T3-2). Acceptance was conceptualized by both a rating scale and unlimited friend nominations. Prompts were identical at each time.

Ratings

Participants were asked to rate how much they liked same-sex peers within their reference group using a five-point Likert scale. Specifically, the reference group within this study was defined as same-sex peers within the participants' main classroom. Higher scores referred to greater liking, whereas lower scores suggested that the adolescent is not well-liked. The rating scale score of acceptance used in this section refers to the number of times an adolescent received a rating of 5 from same-sex peers within their reference group.

Unlimited Nominations

Participants were asked to nominate their same-sex friends within the reference group in order of preference. This was an unlimited choice nomination. Accordingly, the nomination score for this section refers to the number of times a participant was chosen as a first, second, third, and/or other friend from same-sex peers within the reference group. Higher nomination scores reflected the more times they were nominated as a same-sex friend, either first, second, third friend, and/or other friend.

2.6.3 Plan of Analysis

Data analyses we conducted in four steps. First, peer assessment scores for sociometric nominations and sociometric ratings were adjusted for classroom size using a regression-based procedure (see Velásquez et al., 2013). This procedure adjusted the sociometric assessment scores within each same-sex classroom-based reference group such that they would not be biased by class size. Next, to test the strength of the burst design methodology, three mean scores were computed at each of the three waves of data collection (T1, T2, and T3), as described earlier. Pearson bivariate correlations were then computed to assess the associations between the mean scores and single-wave data collection scores. Lastly, statistical differences between correlation coefficients of the burst-wave to single-time scores were assessed using Steiger (1980)'s proposed method of comparing correlated correlations using a Z-score distribution.

2.7 Results

2.7.1 Descriptive Statistics

Sample 1

The rating and nomination scale of peer acceptance remained relatively stable across time. A series of General Linear Models (GLM) were conducted for nomination and peer acceptance separately to assess whether the levels of acceptance changed across time. The estimates were adjusted using the Greenhouse–Geisser correction. The number of times an adolescent received a rating of 5 from same-sex peers ranged between 2.47 and 2.76 ($SD = 1.81$–1.89) across the testing period. Similarly, the number of times an adolescent was chosen as a first, second, third best, and/or other friend from their same-sex peers ranged between 4.84 and 5.10 ($SD = 2.98$–2.23) across time (see Table 1 for descriptive statistics). According to the results for the GLM analysis, the main effect of time was statistically significant for the nominations ($F(4.50, 1,627) = 9.58$, $p < .001$, $\eta p^2 = .026$).

Sample 2

Similar to Sample 1, the rating and nomination scale of peer acceptance remained similar across time. The results from the GLM analyses revealed that the main effect of time was statistically significant ($F(4.50, 1,627) = 9.58$, $p < .001$, $\eta p^2 = .026$). Moreover, a simple contrast revealed that the change was quadratic, $F(1, 350) = 26.35$, $p < .001$, $\eta p^2 = .07$, but small in magnitude. The number of times an adolescent received a rating of 5 from same-sex peers ranged between 2.78 and 3.26 ($SD = 1.94$–1.96).

Table 1 Descriptive statistics of the measures of acceptance by time

Measure	Single						Burst		
	T1-1	T1-2	T2-1	T2-2	T3-1	T3-2	T1	T2	T3
Sample 1									
Nominations									
M (SD)	4.92	5.24	5.18	5.08	5.08	4.88	5.07	5.10	4.84
	(2.05)	(2.09)	(2.19)	(2.04)	(2.06)	(2.02)	(1.98)	(2.06)	(2.23)
Ratings									
M (SD)	2.74	2.78	2.71	2.61	2.47	2.46	2.76	2.66	2.47
	(1.87)	(1.91)	(1.96)	(1.98)	(1.91)	(1.84)	(1.81)	(1.89)	(1.81)
Sample 2									
Nominations									
M (SD)	4.92	4.41	5.15	4.93	5.54	5.76	4.67	5.03	5.65
	(2.17)	(2.39)	(2.02)	(2.09)	(2.10)	(2.04)	(1.96)	(1.92)	(1.88)
Ratings									
M (SD)	3.39	3.13	2.80	2.76	2.82	2.95	3.26	2.79	2.89
	(2.01)	(2.17)	(2.14)	(1.93)	(1.95)	(1.95)	(1.96)	(1.94)	(1.86)

Comparably, the number of times an adolescent was chosen as a first, second, third best, and/or other friend from their same-sex peers ranged between 4.66 and 5.64 (SD = 1.88–1.95) (see Table 1). As evidenced by the GLM analyses, the main effect of time was statistically significant for the friendship nominations $F(4.11, 1439)$ = 15.36, $p < .001$, $\eta p^2 = .042$).

2.7.2 Correlation Comparisons

To determine whether the measurement burst design methodology provided a more stable score of acceptance across time versus a single-time data collection, we computed correlations for each of the single times to their next respective times (i.e., T1-1 to T2-1; T1-2 to T2-2; T2-1 to T3-1, and T2-2 to T3-2) and correlations for the burst times to their successive times (i.e., T1 to T2; T2 to T3) across all three times. Using the Z-score procedure described by Steiger (1980), we compared the corresponding correlations from the burst design to a single-time data collection. For example, the correlation between the nomination scale of acceptance from T1-1 to T2-1 (single time) was compared to the correlation of the nomination scale of acceptance from T1 to T2 (burst design). Table 2 summarizes the correlation matrix for both samples.

With a single exception, across both samples, the correlations across the three times using a measurement burst approach for both the rating scale and nomination scale of acceptance were statistically significantly stronger than the correlations obtained using a single time. The only exception was for Sample 2 at T1-2 to T2-2 where the correlations using a single-time and a burst design did not statistically differ, $p = 0.19$ (see Table 2).

2.8 Summary

In this section, we examined whether a measurement burst design could provide a more stable measure of sociometric assessments relating to peer acceptance across time with two separate adolescent samples. A key feature of our analysis was the capacity to assess the stability of two standard sociometric assessments, namely nominations and ratings of peer acceptance, by comparing the measurement burst coefficients with the single-time assessments across the first three months of the school year. Our hypothesis that measurement bursts would provide stronger estimates was largely supported. Thus, we conclude that this research design is conducive to giving a more precise look at two foundational measurements used in peer research. While this study has notable strengths and weaknesses, the implications of these findings can contribute to our understanding of the psychometric properties of peer acceptance sociometric assessment

Table 2 Comparison of correlation coefficients on measures of acceptance

Correlation Comparison	Z_{obs}	Pearson's r		R^2	
		Single	Burst	Single	Burst
Sample 1					
Nominations					
T1-1/T2-1 versus T1/T2 Burst	-4.82	.77 [.73, .81]	.83 [.79, .86]	0.59	0.69
T1-2/T2-2 versus T1/T2 Burst	-6.09	.75 [.70, .79]	.83 [.79, .86]	0.56	0.69
T2-1/T3-1 versus T2/T3 Burst	-2.41	.81 [.77, .84]	.84 [.81, .87]	0.66	0.71
T2-2/T3-2 versus T2/T3 Burst	-4.31	.77 [.73, .81]	.84 [.81, .87]	0.59	0.71
Ratings					
T1-1/T2-1 versus T1/T2 Burst	-5.43	.75 [.70, .79]	.81 [.77, .84]	0.56	0.66
T1-2/T2-2 versus T1/T2 Burst	-4.23	.76 [.71, .80]	.81 [.77, .84]	0.58	0.66
T2-1/T3-1 versus T2/T3 Burst	-5.53	.80 [.76, .83]	.86 [.83, .88]	0.64	0.74
T2-2/T3-2 versus T2/T3 Burst	-5.18	.80 [.76, .83]	.86 [.83, .88]	0.64	0.74

Table 2 (cont.)

Sample 2					
Nominations					
T1-1/T2-1 versus T1/T2 Burst	−5.39	.70 [.64, .75]	.81 [.77, .84]	0.49	0.66
T1-2/T2-2 versus T1/T2 Burst	−1.29	.79 [.75, .83]	.81 [.77, .84]	0.62	0.66
T2-1/T3-1 versus T2/T3 Burst	−4.85	.57 [.50, .64]	.73 [.68, .77]	0.32	0.53
T2-2/T3-2 versus T2/T3 Burst	−2.66	.65 [.59, .71]	.73 [.68, .78]	0.42	0.53
Ratings					
T1-1/T2-1 versus T1/T2 Burst	−6.11	.68 [.62, .73]	.79 [.75, .83]	0.46	0.62

scores and their use within the peer relations domain while addressing limitations to the current literature.

Our analyses revealed two main findings that were consistent across both samples. First, both the rating and nomination measure of peer acceptance remained stable across the testing period. Although adolescent peer relations are both complex and multidimensional in nature, the developmental trajectory of peer acceptance is known to be relatively stable and linear (Cillessen & Borche, 2006; Jiang & Cillessen, 2005), which is supported by our results. Second, employing a measurement burst design methodology produced more stable sociometric assessment scores, both for the rating and nomination measures of peer acceptance, in two distinct adolescent samples when compared with a single-time design. The only exclusion was in Sample 2 for the correlation between T1-2 and T2-2 where the stability of peer nominations using the measurement burst did not differ statistically to the stability of peer nominations using the single-time design. While this discrepancy could potentially be chalked up to a statistical artifact, it can also potentially demonstrate that friendships may be more stable at the beginning of the school year within this particular sample specifically. This single exception within two separate adolescent samples speaks to the strength of our results. Additionally, we were able to replicate the finding that a measurement burst design creates a more stable measure of acceptance using sociometric assessments in two separate adolescent samples. It appears that multiple bursts of measurement spread by a longer interval may curtail the effects of intraindividual variability to ensure that the phenomenon of peer acceptance as assessed by sociometric assessments is more accurately captured as a construct. Specifically, while identifying interindividual variability is a fundamental component in developmental research, the measurement burst design can be a useful tool at obtaining a measure of global experiences relating to peer acceptance. Moreover, while childhood and adolescence are marked by the ability to create voluntary intimate relationships with others, peer relations can change as goals, motivations, and needs vary (Poulin & Chan, 2010). Similarly, a meta-analytic study found that sociometric nominations of peer acceptance are influenced by both age of the participants and interval length of the study (Jiang & Cillessen, 2005). Specifically, as age of the participants and interval length of the longitudinal study increase, the stability of sociometric nominations decreases (Bukowski & Newcomb, 1983). Similarly, interval length significantly moderated the stability of sociometric ratings such that scores were less stable as interval length increased (Jiang & Cillessen, 2005). This has direct relevance to adolescent well-being. Specifically, sociometric assessments of peer acceptance (and rejection) are useful tools for not only assessing intervention effects but also identifying youth that are at risk or in risky relationships (Cillessen & Marks, 2011). Accordingly, ensuring stability of sociometric assessments should be paramount in peer relations research. Moreover, while interval lengths of a study and participant age are well established factors that moderate findings within developmental research, we were able to demonstrate that the measurement burst design resulted in a more stable measure for peer ratings and nominations of acceptance. Thus, we speculate that the use of multiple data collections nested within longitudinal designs across longer intervals could minimize the effect of age and study interval length on the stability of sociometric assessments. In particular, we speculate that having multiple measures of the same construct within a longitudinal study may reduce unwanted variability in sociometric assessment scores.

2.9 Strengths, Limitations, and Future Directions

While this section has several notable strengths such as the novelty of using a measurement burst design methodology to assess the stability of peer acceptance within two distinct adolescent samples, it is not without its limitations. As previously outlined, the constructs of acceptance and popularity are distinct but interrelated. Although the overlap between acceptance and popularity decreases exponentially in early adolescence, future work would benefit from examining the developmental trajectory of acceptance and popularity scores in tandem across the lifespan using a burst design methodology in order to not only reduce variance created construct overlap, but also to minimize the effects of participant age and study interval length on the stability of these aforementioned scores.

To our knowledge, longitudinal changes in sociometric assessments of peer acceptance using a burst design measurement methodology have not yet been investigated. Particularly with sociometric assessments, developmental researchers should be interested in examining short- and long-term stability of sociometric assessments, given the different conclusions that can be drawn from each type of analysis (Jiang & Cillessen, 2005). With regards to short-term stability, the test-retest reliability of the sociometric assessment can be investigated (Jiang & Cillessen, 2005), as can fluctuations in peer experiences that may alter an adolescent's standing within the peer group. Conversely, regarding long-term stability, the developmental trajectory of peer acceptance as a phenomenon in development can be better understood and explored using the measurement burst design to determine how different social behavioral correlates influence peer acceptance across the lifespan (Jiang & Cillessen, 2005). Despite its more common use with adult populations (e.g., Lee et al., 2018), there are multiple avenues for future research to explore the utility of measurement burst designs across younger samples and different constructs.

Finally, it is important to note the implications associated with sociometric assessments. In particular, peer ratings and nominations are a useful tool not only to assess for intervention effects but also to identify youth that are in problematic peer relations. While acceptance is typically associated with positive outcomes relating to having higher emotional intelligence and socio-cognitive skills (McDonald & Asher, 2018; Newcomb et al., 1993), peer rejection is coupled with potentially detrimental negative consequences on the well-being of the child such as being victimized by their peers (Zimmer-Gembeck, 2016). Having a more stable measure of sociometric assessments, not only in the context of acceptance, can have great implications for testing interventions and identifying at-risk youth, which is directly related to promoting well-being in adolescence.

3 Experiences with Social and Test Anxiety

A central feature of theory about well-being in early adolescence is the claim that experiences with anxiety can be moderated by positive friendships (Sullivan, 1953). Although this period of the lifespan is marked by increased social pressures and comparisons, findings illustrate the well-known protective effect that peers can have on anxiety across the school year (e.g., Wood et al., 2017). However, for those who experience difficulties within their peer groups, anxiety can emerge and put youth at risk for developing other forms of anxiety and/or comorbid problems, as well as have a negative impact on their functioning both at home and at school (Hong et al., 2017). Studies comparing youth living with anxiety compared to their non-anxious peers have demonstrated that anxious children tend to exhibit a heightened level of negative affect and sensitivity in situations that present little or no threat, and lack confidence in their abilities to cope with and regulate their negative emotional state (e.g., Woodgate et al., 2020). Nonetheless, it is important to consider that the day-to day experiences of early adolescents may vary over time given the many contexts in which they function. As such, we argue in the present section that the degree of variability across common experiences in adolescence is critical to consider when the measurement of important psychological constructs, such as anxiety, is concerned.

3.1 Anxiety as a Multidimensional Construct

Anxiety is a unidimensional construct. It is composed of maladaptive processes that interact to affect the various ways in which symptoms can be experienced, manifested, and maintained (Barlow et al., 2014). Specifically, prominent models of anxiety suggest that it is made up of three largely interrelated components: (1) cognitive, which involves one's subjective interpretation of internal and external stimuli, (2) physiological, which refers to an individual's internal state, and (3), behavioural, which is how one responds to these stimuli. Although longitudinal studies have demonstrated that symptoms of anxiety remain relatively stable over time in youth across a three-year period (Gullone et al., 2001), as well as from early childhood through adolescence (Bosquet & Egeland, 2006), there are important developmental differences in the expression and continuation of anxiety symptoms across age groups that should be considered (e.g., Field & Lester, 2010). For example, school-age children are typically less sophisticated in their coping and avoidance strategies, which may lead them to externalize their symptoms, thus displaying more overt signs of anxiety which can include somatic complaints (e.g., stomach aches, headaches), irritability, nail biting, inattentiveness, and distractibility (Muris et al., 2008). Due to the limitations in their cognitive development, younger children may have difficulty accurately labeling and identifying their anxious thoughts, feelings, and worries. Whereas symptoms of generalized anxiety are less frequent among younger children, they tend to become more apparent in early adolescence (Broeren & Murris, 2009). As a result of the developmental changes that occur during the transition between childhood and adolescence, children's cognitive capacities become increasingly developed, and their fears may start to revolve around anticipatory events and more abstract stimuli (Gullone, 2000). Thus, cognitive vulnerabilities to anxiety such as worry can emerge and play an important role in the early teenage years.

In addition to the fact that the interplay between the cognitive and physiological components of anxiety can be very distressing for a young adolescent, this developmental period is also a time characterized by many biological, social and cognitive changes which pose unique challenges (Nelemans et al., 2017). Teenagers who are unable to effectively cope with the changes and uncertainties associated with the onset of adolescence are at an increased risk for experiencing levels of anxiety that may interfere in their participation in various social and academic opportunities (McEvoy & Mahoney, 2012). For instance, youth with heightened levels of anxiety may worry about seemingly mundane tasks and events, such as their performance at school or in other activities and may be hypervigilant to slight changes in their social relationships. It is also possible that anxious youth worry more about their health and that of their close others, and about other unpredictable events out of their control that could have implications on their overall well-being (Woodgate et al., 2020).

3.2 Social and Test Anxiety as Common Experiences among Young Adolescents

Child mental health is markedly influenced by the peer system, which begins to play an integral role in childhood and early adolescence as children become peer- rather than family-centered (Rubin et al., 2006). Adolescents and their peers function in many contexts including the social and academic domains, with children typically spending up to half of their waking hours at school (Nelemans et al., 2017; Silver et al., 2010). As such, the pressures of performing well academically and maintaining positive relationships with peers and teachers can be critical to feelings of self-worth and overall well-being, with some children becoming hypersensitive to criticisms and approval by their peers (Silver et al., 2010).

Relatedly, it is well documented that anxiety can be context-dependent, such that it might be more pronounced in one situation relative to another (Carleton, 2016). Specifically, while the degree of uncertainty can be similar across two separate settings, an individual may feel more comfortable and competent and believe that they possess the adequate skills to be able to respond in one context more effectively (e.g., social situations) compared to another (e.g., testing situations). Despite this important consideration, items found across common childhood measures of anxiety (e.g., Multidimensional Anxiety Scale for Children – Second Edition [MASC-2; March, 2013]) lack contextual specificity and breadth. While the measures are designed to differentiate between different types of anxiety (e.g., social anxiety, separation anxiety, phobia), the items themselves fail to include context-specific information, which can make it especially challenging for a child to relate to the items being presented. This may also prevent investigators from acquiring important information regarding whether a child is generally anxious across all contexts, or more anxious in one context relative to another.

To address this limitation, this section seeks to assess children's anxiety in two developmentally salient contexts: (a) socially and (b) academically. Individuals with social anxiety typically present with negative thoughts prior to, during, and after social interactions or socially evaluative circumstances (Hearn et al., 2017). Often, these negatively valenced thoughts and worries pertain to how others perceive them and their behaviours, and how they perceive themselves during social situations. On the other hand, young adolescents with heightened feelings of test anxiety typically feel tense, afraid, and worried when confronted with evaluative situations, which can have a negative impact on their learning and overall academic performance (Spielberger & Vagg, 1995; Sub & Prabha, 2003). In accordance with a cognitive-attentional model of test anxiety, students may experience an influx of task-relevant (e.g., worries about the self and one's performance), as well as task-irrelevant thoughts and worries, which can interfere with one's ability to focus, resulting in physiological hyperarousal and either adaptive (e.g., studying more for a test) or maladaptive behaviours (e.g., skipping items) (Wigfield & Eccles, 1989; Wine, 1971).

3.3 Measuring Anxiety

Across research and clinical practice, the most commonly used and preferred method of assessing early adolescents' affective experiences involves obtaining respondents' subjective reports via self-report measures. As illustrated by Berne and colleagues (2013), self-report questionnaires have several advantages compared to other methods in that they allow researchers to collect large amounts of data in a relatively short period of time and at a low cost. Also, self-report measures are simple to administer and are quick for respondents to complete. This is especially valuable in the context of longitudinal studies where researchers must maximize participants' time and level of engagement. Importantly, self-report questionnaires allow researchers to obtain information about one's private experiences, which may be missed by peers, teachers, and/or parents (Thomas et al., 2015).

Across the anxiety literature, studies typically employ longitudinal designs in an effort to track changes in anxiety across time, or a pre-post design where symptoms are measured before and after the administration of a specific treatment (e.g., Kerns et al., 2013; Nelemans et al., 2017). While both these methodological designs are effective ways of assessing change or stability, they fail to fully consider intraindividual variabilities in human behaviour (e.g., Fiske & Rice, 1955). Given what is known about anxiety and the influence of environmental factors (e.g., context), relying on a single measurement at two separate times may not be entirely representative of an individual's true or "general" level of anxiety. For instance, when collecting data within individual classrooms, it is highly possible that students may have either had or will have an exam, which can significantly affect levels of test anxiety. Similarly, as social anxiety scores are concerned, it could be that an interpersonal event took place at school the day of the data collection (e.g., group project, disagreement with a peer), which could have affected a child's overall level of social anxiety. Thus, we argue that a measurement burst design, which incorporates the benefits of both a longitudinal and short-term within-person level of analysis, is a more effective and precise way of assessing changes in anxiety levels across time, given that it addresses the difficulties that arise when measuring variables that can fluctuate as a result of daily experiences.

3.4 Goals of This Section

In this section, our aim is to demonstrate that a burst design methodology provides a more accurate, stable, and reliable measurement of young adolescents' internalizing symptoms of social and test anxiety. Specifically, we hypothesize that a longitudinal design with three bursts, each with two assessments, will demonstrate superior levels of internal consistency and measurement stability when compared to a single-time longitudinal design using two separate samples of early adolescents. The data collection took place at three separate waves (Time 1: T1, Time 2: T2, and Time 3: T3). Within each wave or burst of assessment, two assessments were collected, separated by one week, which produced six different observations for each participant.

3.5 Method

3.5.1 Participants

Two samples of data were used in which the burst design format was employed to assess self-reported levels of anxiety. In this section, participants from Sample 2 ($N = 351$) and Sample 3 ($N = 164$) (described earlier) were included in the analyses.

3.5.2 Measures

At each of the six assessment times, participants rated items designed to assess anxiety in both the social and test contexts using a five-point scale with endpoints *never* (1) and *almost always* (5). Higher scores on each of these items indicated higher levels of anxiety. Participants were instructed to indicate how much each statement generally describes them and were not provided with specific windows of reference (e.g., in the past week, month).

Social Anxiety

In both samples, the same three items were used to measure social anxiety within each burst, at all three times: (1) "I can feel nervous when I am with other kids in my class"; (2) "I worry about what other people might think of me"; and (3) "Sometimes I am afraid that some people in my class might make fun of me."

Test anxiety

Using a five-point scale with endpoints *never* (1) and *almost always* (5), children in Sample 1 and Sample 2 rated three identical items that were designed to assess levels of test anxiety within each burst at each time: (1) "I worry about not doing well in a test in school"; (2) "I get nervous before I have to take a test in class"; and (3) "After I take a test I worry a lot about how I did on it."

3.5.3 Plan of Analysis

Data analyses were conducted in three steps. First, within each sample, mean scores were then computed in order to represent participant scores at different times (see Table 3 for descriptive statistics). As described earlier, three mean scores were created at each of the three waves of data collection, yielding a total of nine mean scores within the social anxiety domain, and nine mean scores within the test anxiety domain. Six of the nine scores represented the mean of all participating students' scores at each of the six assessment times. In order to assess the strength of the burst design format, three additional mean scores were computed which represented the combination of scores from assessments 1 and 2 within each assessment (i.e., T1, T2, T3). Third, Pearson bivariate correlations were computed to assess the associations between the nine mean scores within each domain (see Table 3). The final set of analyses involved testing the statistical difference between correlation coefficients, based on a Z-score comparison test, as suggested by Steiger (1980).

3.6 Results

3.6.1 Descriptive Statistics

Mean Scores

In the first set of analyses, mean scores of social anxiety and test anxiety were used to (1) compare overall levels of anxiety across both domains of functioning and (2) to assess the degree of stability of each form of anxiety over time. Test anxiety scores were observed to be consistently higher compared to scores on measures of social anxiety among both samples of participants, with mean levels ranging from 2.83 to 3.43 for test anxiety, and from 2.18 to 2.50 for social anxiety (see Table 3). To examine mean-level changes across time, a series of Generalized Linear Models (GLM) were estimated separately for each type of anxiety and sample (estimated adjusted using the Greenhouse–Geisser correction). The results from models that included the six assessments times revealed that the main effect of time was not statistically significant for social anxiety in any of the samples (Sample 2: $F(3.39, 373) = 2.1, p = .09, \eta p^2 = .02$; Sample 3: $F(4.53, 1,589) = 1.35, p = .24, \eta p^2 = .004$). When the GLM were estimated including the three bursts, the results revealed the presence of a statistically significant main effect of time for social anxiety in Sample 2, $F(1.74, 276) = 5.42, p = .01, \eta p^2 = .03$, but not on

Table 3 Descriptive statistics and reliability of the measures of anxiety by time

Measure	Single						Burst		
	T1-1	T1-2	T2-1	T2-2	T3-1	T3-2	T1	T2	T3
Sample 2									
Social Anxiety									
M (SD)	2.50 (1.04)	2.46 (1.11)	2.38 (1.11)	2.38 (1.15)	2.18 (1.08)	2.29 (1.10)	2.48 (.98)	2.38 (1.06)	2.24 (1.05)
α	.79 [.72, .84]	.82 [.76, .87]	.80 [.73, .85]	.84 [.79, .88]	.89 [.85, .92]	.88 [.85, .91]	.87 [.82, .89]	.89 [.85, .91]	.93 [.92, .95]
Within-level ω							.82	.84	.89
Between-level ω							.90	.88	.84
Test Anxiety									
M (SD)	3.27 (1.07)	3.00 (1.20)	2.96 (1.13)	2.95 (1.19)	2.83 (1.10)	2.84 (1.21)	3.14 (1.05)	2.95 (1.09)	2.83 (1.09)
α	.81 [.75, .85]	.87 [.83, .91]	.83 [.78, .88]	.88 [.84, .91]	.87 [.83, .90]	.92 [.90, .94]	.89 [.87, .92]	.91 [.88, .93]	.93 [.91, .95]

Table 3 (cont.)

Within-level ω							.84	.86	.90
Between-level ω							.98	.86	.83
Sample 3									
Social Anxiety									
M (SD)	2.45	2.36	2.43	2.40	2.37	2.47	2.40	2.42	2.42
	(1.12)	(1.15)	(1.18)	(1.14)	(1.18)	(1.18)	(1.03)	(1.05)	(1.08)
α	.73	.77	.83	.82	.86	.86	.84	.87	.89
	[.68, .78]	[.73, .81]	[.79, .86]	[.78, .85]	[.83, .88]	[.86, .84]	[.81, .86]	[.85, .89]	[.87, .91]
Within-level ω							.76	.83	.86
Between-level ω							.95	.93	.95
Test Anxiety									
M (SD)	3.43	3.28	3.35	3.20	3.25	3.15	3.35	3.27	3.20
	(1.04)	(1.19)	(1.09)	(1.21)	(1.17)	(1.24)	(1.01)	(1.06)	(1.11)
α	.72	.83	.80	.86	.86	.90	.85	.88	.91
	[.67, .77]	[.80, .86]	[.76, .83]	[.83, .88]	[.83, .88]	[.88, .91]	[.83, .87]	[.86, .90]	[.89, .92]
Within-level ω							.79	.83	.88
Between-level ω							.99	.99	.99

Sample 3, $F(1.89, 670) = .05$, $p = .94$, $\eta p^2 = .001$). As displayed in Table 3, social anxiety as measured by the burst design seemed to decrease with time, although this effect was small in magnitude. Regarding test anxiety, the GLM that included six measurement times revealed that the main effect of time was statistically significant for test anxiety in both samples (Sample 2: $F(3.91, 430) = 6.39$, $p < .001$, $\eta p^2 = .06$; Sample 3: $F(4.39, 1,536) = 6.69$, $p < .001$, $\eta p^2 = .02$). The same result was observed with the GLM that included the three bursts (Sample 2: $F(1.92, 306) = 13.83$, $p < .001$, $\eta p^2 = .08$; Sample 3: $F(1.85, 649) = 5.94$, $p = .01$, $\eta p^2 = .02$). As displayed in Table 3, test anxiety tended to decrease with time, although this effect was small in magnitude.

3.6.2 Internal Consistency and Multilevel Reliability

The next set of analyses evaluated the degree of internal consistency among the measures of anxiety in both the social and test domains, across the two samples. Social anxiety scores and test anxiety scores demonstrated good levels of internal consistency at all three waves of assessment, with Cronbach's α ranging from .73 to .93, and .72 to .93, respectively. Greater levels of internal consistency were observed among the combined burst scores compared to the single burst scores. Next, we evaluated these scales using multilevel reliability which was assessed at each of the three times. For social anxiety, we found that the within-level ω ranged between .82 and .89 for Sample 2 and between .76 and .86 for Sample 3. The between-level ω was between .84 and .90 for Sample 2 and between .93 and .95 for Sample 3. Regarding test anxiety, within-level ω estimates were between .84 and .90 for Sample 2, and between .79 and .88 for Sample 3, whereas the between-level ω ranged from .83 to .98 for Sample 2 and was .99 at each time in Sample 3. Descriptive statistics calculated for these two measures of anxiety and their respective alphas at each time are presented in Table 3.

3.6.3 Correlation Comparisons

The goal of the final set of analyses was to determine whether the measurement burst design, which combines the two measurements at each burst, demonstrated superior levels of stability for both measures of anxiety compared to data used from a single time. To do this, correlation coefficients observed using the measurement burst design format and those obtained using data from a single time at each of the three times were compared using Steiger's (1980) correlation comparison technique. When Pearson bivariate correlations were compared between the nine mean scores within each domain (social and test), analyses revealed that the across-time correlations among the combined burst measures were greater compared to the correlation coefficients of single-time measures across time (see Table 4). All but one of the observed Z-scores assessing change from T1 to T2 and T2 to T3 were observed to be statistically significant, surpassing the critical value of 1.96 in both domains of functioning (see Table 4). The Z-score representing the difference between T2 and T3 levels of social anxiety in Sample 2 when using a measurement burst design versus data from a single time was observed to be statistically nonsignificant ($Z_{obs} = -1.61$, $p = .053$). Briefly, evidence obtained across all analyses suggests that the measurement burst design demonstrates stronger estimates of stability and reliability among both samples of participants when compared to data drawn from a single time point.

3.7 Summary

The primary aim of this section was to demonstrate the benefits of using a measurement burst design when assessing change and stability over time in internalizing symptoms among youth. Our findings suggest that when compared to a longitudinal design employing a single data collection point, the measurement burst demonstrated superior levels of internal consistency and measurement stability on measures of social and test anxiety.

First, we hypothesized that measures of social and test anxiety would be more reliable when two successive data collections were combined to produce one mean score, compared to the use of a single data point at each wave of assessment. Analyses provided broad support for this hypothesis, in that measures of social and test anxiety at all three times demonstrated greater levels of internal consistency when the measurement burst design method was used. While one could argue that this finding may be due to the fact that the same items were used across time and that reliability increases as the number of items that make up the scale also increases (Torabi, 1994), the measurement burst design's ability to account for intraindividual variability via the multilevel reliability estimates still supports its utility.

In addition, our hypothesis that mean levels of anxiety obtained using the measurement burst design method would provide better indices of change across time compared to scores derived from a single time point also was supported. Specifically, a statistically significant difference was observed between the strength of the across-time associations of both forms of anxiety when comparing the correlation coefficients obtained using a burst design and those obtained with a traditional longitudinal framework, with the measurement burst design demonstrating stronger associations across the three times. Importantly, all the observed Z-scores, with one exception, surpassed the critical

Table 4 Comparison of correlation coefficients on measures of anxiety

Correlation Comparison	Z_{obs}	Pearson's r			R^2	
		Single	Burst		Single	Burst
Sample 2						
Social Anxiety						
T1-1/T2-1 versus T1/T2 Burst	−4.81	.63 [.53, .71]	.77 [.70, .82]		0.40	0.59
T1-2/T2-2 versus T1/T2 Burst	−3.71	.67 [.58, .74]	.77 [.70, .82]		0.45	0.59
T2-1/T3-1 versus T2/T3 Burst	−1.61	.76 [.69, .82]	.79 [.73, .84]		0.58	0.62
T2-2/T3-2 versus T2/T3 Burst	−3.72	.72 [.64, .78]	.79 [.73, .84]		0.52	0.62
Test Anxiety						
T1-1/T2-1 versus T1/T2 Burst	−3.92	.65 [.56, .73]	.75 [.68, .81]		0.42	0.56
T1-2/T2-2 versus T1/T2 Burst	−3.30	.67 [.58, .74]	.75 [.68, .81]		0.45	0.56
T2-1/T3-1 versus T2/T3 Burst	−4.18	.70 [.62, .77]	.80 [.74, .85]		0.49	0.64
T2-2/T3-2 versus T2/T3 Burst	−3.94	.71 [.63, .78]	.80 [.74, .85]		0.50	0.64

Table 4 (cont.)

Sample 3					
Social Anxiety					
T1-1/T2-1 versus T1/T2 Burst	−3.21	.64 [.57, .70]	.71 [.61, .76]	0.41	0.50
T1-2/T2-2 versus T1/T2 Burst	−7.11	.54 [.46, .61]	.71 [.61, .76]	0.29	0.50
T2-1/T3-1 versus T2/T3 Burst	−6.76	.61 [.54, .67]	.76 [.71, .80]	0.37	0.58
T2-2/T3-2 versus T2/T3 Burst	−4.76	.66 [.60, .72]	.76 [.71, .80]	0.44	0.58
Test Anxiety					
T1-1/T2-1 versus T1/T2 Burst	−4.13	.58 [.51, .65]	.68 [.62, .73]	0.34	0.46
T1-2/T2-2 versus T1/T2 Burst	−4.93	.57 [.50, .64]	.68 [.62, .73]	0.32	0.46
T2-1/T3-1 versus T2/T3 Burst	−4.88	.67 [.61, .72]	.77 [.72, .81]	0.45	0.59
T2-2/T3-2 versus T2/T3 Burst	−6.50	.64 [.57, .70]	.77 [.72, .81]	0.41	0.59

value of 1.96 (assuming an alpha of 0.05), which speaks to the strength of our findings. While the Z-score correlation comparison calculation (Steiger, 1980) did not demonstrate a statistically significant difference across measures of social anxiety from T2 to T3 for Sample 2 only, it did appear as a trend, and we argue that it still provides support for our initial hypothesis. Specifically, the obtained Z-score of −1.61 would be on the verge of significance if a less rigorous cut-off value were used ($p = 0.053$). In light of these findings, it is evident that multiple bursts of measurement minimize the impact of within-person variability and ensure that scores obtained on measures of psychological constructs are accurate reflections of each participant's true level of the construct rather than their level at one very specific moment in time (McHale et al., 2014). While this was the objective of the present section, some studies may wish to assess the within-person fluctuations across variables. Thus, it is worth noting that the measurement burst method should be used in accordance with each study's specific design and objectives. Given what is known about internalizing symptoms and their tendency to fluctuate as a result of environmental factors, our findings provide further support for the use of assessing change in psychological constructs using a measurement burst design.

With regards to the differences in the individual trajectories of social and test anxiety across the academic year, our analyses revealed greater mean levels of test anxiety compared to levels of social anxiety among both samples of participants. While our analyses showed that both measures of anxiety were consistent over time, mean levels of test anxiety generally decreased across the three times, whereas mean levels of social anxiety remained relatively consistent in both samples. These findings are in line with previous literature in that studies report a stable pattern of social anxiety symptoms across adolescence (e.g., Danneel et al., 2020; Nelemans et al., 2014). In considering test anxiety scores, although there is much uncertainty with regards to a teacher's preferred format for administering examinations at the beginning of the school year, this becomes more predictable as the year progresses. With time, students become better acquainted with their teacher's exam style, organization and expectations, and their previous test-taking experiences likely serve to minimize anxiety and increase both self-confidence and overall performance (Wigfield & Eccles, 1989). Thus, this may serve to explain why mean levels of test anxiety were found to decrease across time in our data.

3.8 Strengths, Limitations, and Future Directions

To our knowledge, longitudinal changes in various forms of anxiety using a measurement burst design methodology in two large community samples of preadolescents has not yet been investigated. Given that the application of the measurement burst design has mostly been used across studies with adult participants (e.g., Lee et al., 2018), we argue that this should become more common practice across developmental research.

The use of the measurement burst design encompasses the benefits of longitudinal and short-term within-person levels of analysis by allowing us to assess developmental changes in internalizing symptoms across the academic school year with more precision and reliability. Understanding the developmental trajectory of anxiety among youth is crucial as it can be an important indicator of problematic anxiety and other comorbid problems that may emerge later on (Broeren et al., 2013). However, this can be facilitated only if proper measurement techniques are used which minimize the potential influences of external circumstances that can occur at any given moment, that serve to inflate or exaggerate levels of anxiety. The application of the measurement burst design in our research minimizes this possibility and thus is a major strength of the present investigation.

Although this study has many strengths, it is not without its limitations. It should be considered that while anxiety is a multidimensional construct, the measure used in this section to assess both levels of social and test anxiety captured only the cognitive component of anxiety known as worry (Fialko et al., 2012). Thus, future work would benefit from implementing a measure of anxiety that also captures the physiological and physical components to ensure that the experience of anxiety among youth is captured fully. Also, given that anxiety and depressed affect are often comorbid (Hong et al., 2017), future investigations should control for the effects of depressed affect as a potential influence on self-reports of anxiety. Another avenue for future research would be to examine how the burst design method would relate to the assessment of other psychological constructs, and to assess how relationship factors experienced at each burst of assessment, such as security and intimacy among friendships, can influence the trajectory of internalizing symptoms.

The present findings are particularly relevant to both the theoretical and practical domains. Beyond providing further empirical support for the stability of two forms of anxiety among early adolescents, the current study highlights the advantages of using the measurement burst design when assessing psychological constructs. Our findings also have important practical implications for the treatment of anxiety among youth in that the within-person information that is made available via the use of the measurement burst method provides unique information with respect to the targets and timing of interventions (Smyth et al., 2017). Specifically, the measurement burst method allows for each individual to serve as his or her own control, and as such, various antecedents and processes that can affect an individual's mental health trajectory can be identified and targeted in treatment, enhancing the effectiveness of the intervention.

4 Assessing Domain-Specific Features of the Self-Concept

Self-concept can be defined as the way individuals "perceive, experience, and think about their own features, existence, and functioning in the past, present, and future" (Bukowski & Raufelder, 2018, p. 144). Broadly speaking, it is characterized as being multidimensional in nature, such that individuals are capable of conceiving multiple *versions* of themselves in a variety of life domains (e.g., social, physical, romantic, academic) beyond having a general sense of self (Harter, 2006). Longitudinal studies that make use of single time measures spaced by at least one year have found that the self-concept tends to be stable across the lifespan (Cole et al. 2001; Huang, 2010; Kuster & Orth, 2013). This conception of the self as static and unchangeable seems incompatible with previous conceptualizations that acknowledge the potential influence of social interactions on the development of the self. For instance, references to social or interpersonal attributes to describe the self (e.g., "*I am nice to others*") become more common during early adolescence (Harter, 2012; Setoh et al., 2015). Indeed, by sharing relational contexts such as school, adolescents can confirm, disconfirm, or change the ideas, benchmarks, and feelings they have about themselves (Bukowski et al., 2015).

The paradox of the self as being highly stable but also susceptible to change in social interactions might be explained by the traditional design of longitudinal studies. Although meta-analyses including all of the developmental stages have found that mean level changes in self-concept are not impacted by the length of time interval between data collections (Harris & Orth, 2020; Huang, 2010), this conclusion applies only to studies with at least a one-year interval between assessments. Unfortunately, shorter time periods between data collections have not received an equivalent attention in the literature, and most of the existing studies on this topic focus on adult samples (Alessandri et al., 2013; Fortes et al., 2004). Similarly, the evidence regarding fluctuations of self-concept in younger samples during shorter time periods is limited and inconclusive. While some studies have documented important daily fluctuations (Morrow et al., 2019); others do not appear to find evidence of variability of self-concept across days (Hank & Baltes-Götz, 2019). This section aims to demonstrate the short-time stability of the self-concept by the use of a measurement burst design, when measures were spaced by one week apart across three times.

The importance of examining fluctuations in self-concept in shorter time periods is especially relevant in early adolescence for three reasons. First, the changing nature of social relationships, which is typical during this stage of life, might influence the conception of individuals about themselves. For instance, young adolescents who were asked to report daily measures of social self-concept and victimization over the course of eight school days reported lower levels of social self-concept on days when they perceived higher victimization (Morrow et al., 2019). In contrast, when adolescents reported on their self-esteem three times a day during a two-day period in a sample, the variations were minimal (Hank & Balter-Götz, 2019). Second, during the transition between childhood and adolescence, the cognitive capacity to engage in social comparisons, such as engaging in self-evaluations of one's performance and characteristics against another person's performance and characteristics, becomes more sophisticated (Festinger, 1954). As suggested by Harter (2006), by comparing themselves with their peers, young adolescents confirm or disconfirm their ideas about themselves. Finally, at this age individuals are capable of conceiving different "versions" of themselves in physical, academic, romantic, vocational, and social domains (Harter, 2012). Relatedly, they can consider, simultaneously, both positive and negative dimensions of their competence on those domains (Harter, 2006). Based on the aforementioned reasons, this section explores the stability of general positive, general negative, and social positive domains of self-concept in a sample of early adolescents. These domains are analyzed within short time periods between assessments in an effort to shed light on to the development of the self-concept among early adolescents.

4.1 Positive, Negative, and Social Dimensions

The existing research on adolescent self-concept is primarily based on its positive valence. Moreover, multiple terms have been used in the literature to describe individuals' positive perceptions about themselves, such as *self-esteem*, *perceived competence*, and *self-worth* (Byrne, 1996). For purposes of consistency, we use *positive self-concept* to collectively represent these terms in this section. Overall, findings suggest that having a positive self-concept is beneficial. For example, individuals who possess a positive view of themselves tend to also have more supportive social relationships in adolescence (Marshall et al., 2014) and a better overall physical health in adulthood (Orth et al., 2012). Conversely, having a more positive self-concept is also negatively associated with psychological outcomes such as depressive affect (Klima & Repeti, 2008).

Despite the broad consensus among researchers about the multidimensional nature of the self-concept, the current literature is limited in its operationalization as a continuum between positive and negative valences. A more appropriate approach to the study and measurement of the self needs to acknowledge the existence of a two-factor structure, in which individuals can have positive *and* negative views of themselves simultaneously (Bukowski & Raufelder, 2018). For instance, longitudinal work spanning from adolescence to young adulthood showed that the factorial structure of self-esteem with two distinct dimensions that reflected positive and negative self-esteem was more appropriate than a model with a single factor (Owens, 1993). Moreover, this two-factor model was consistent (i.e., structurally invariant) across time, whereas the single-factor solution was not (Owens, 1993). To our knowledge, self-concept has not been measured from a two-factor perspective in samples of young adolescents, with the exception of Owens (1993). As a result, evidence about the negative self-perceptions at this developmental stage remains scarce. In this section, we also considered the negative dimension of the self in addition to the traditional positive valence that is well established within the existing literature.

In addition to having general positive and negative views about themselves, individuals are capable of differentiating the self across multiple domains (Harter, 2006). Since positive associations between self-concept and social interactions seem to be reciprocal and consistent among different stages of life and relational partners (e.g., peers, parents) (see Harris & Orth, 2020 for a review), we also included items to assess the social self-concept. In general, social self-concept is defined as the evaluation of one's own competence to start, maintain, and experience positive social interactions with others (Harter, 2012). Not only are social exchanges a fundamental part of the construction of the social self-concept, but the social self also influences the way adolescents approach and behave toward others. Evidence from prior studies, for example, show that high levels of perceived social competence are associated with higher levels of peer acceptance (Gest et al., 2005). In contrast, certain forms of victimization such as bullying (Boulton, et al., 2010) and exclusion (Morrow et al., 2019) can negatively impact one's social self-concept, thus decreasing an individual's perception of their skills to effectively and successfully engage in social relationships.

4.2 The Measurement of Self-Concept

One of the most common scales to assess self-concept in childhood and adolescence is the Children's Perceived Competence Scale (Harter, 1982, 1985). In recent updates to the scale, separate questionnaires are considered for each developmental stage, such as the *Self-Perception Profile for*

Adolescents (Harter, 1988, 2012). This scale assesses global self-worth, as well as domain-specific subscales including social, cognitive, and physical self-concept among others (Harter 1988, 2012). Items are presented as pairs of descriptions, one positive and one negative (e.g., "Some teenagers are happy with themselves most of the time *but* other teenagers are often not happy with themselves"), and subjects are asked to choose the teenager from the item with whom they identify more with (Harter, 1988, 2012). These items are rated dichotomously, such that participants report if the chosen description is either "sort of true" or "really true" for them. Higher scores on items reflect higher levels of self-competence. The scale has been validated in diverse samples and has shown acceptable levels of internal consistency (Harter, 1988, 2012).

Although Harter assessed the self-concept as a multidimensional construct, the scoring system of this scale hinders its negative valence. Specifically, if individuals choose the negative description over the positive, their score on that item is coded as 1 if the answer is "really true for me" and as 2 if the answer is "sort of true for me" (Harter 1988, 2012). Next, all the items that correspond to each dimension are averaged into a single estimate for each domain. Under this scoring system, the experience of a strong negative perception about the self is represented as the low level of a positive perception. Although a negative association between positive and negative valences is expected, this scoring procedure assumes that this association is linear and almost perfect, and does not, however, acknowledge the possibility of the simultaneous coexistence of positive and negative perceptions about the self.

As a consequence, the existing conclusions about low levels of self-concept could be mistakenly interpreted as conclusions about its negative valence. In contrast, a more accurate view could be one that measures two dimensions of self-concept, namely the positive and negative perspectives, within each sub-domain. The close association between affect and an individual's perceptions about themselves illustrates this idea. In a sample of youth ranging between 9 and 13 years old, Nelis and Bukowski (2019) observed that the bivariate correlations between self-esteem (measured as positive self-concept) and two dimensions of affect varied in magnitude, the one with positive affect being stronger than the one with negative affect (.53 and -.23 respectively). Owens (1993) found similar results in an older sample of tenth graders when exploring the associations between depressed affect and two dimensions of self-concept (i.e., self-confidence and self-deprecation). Building on these findings, we measured positive and negative self-concept dimensions separately.

4.3 Goals of this Section

This section aims to describe the stability of positive, negative, and positive social dimensions of self-concept, using data collected at different times within a school year in a sample of young adolescents. We hypothesized that the use of measurement bursts would result in estimates with higher levels of reliability and between-time stability when compared to estimates obtained using single time measurements. A second purpose of this section is to explore the associations between positive, negative, and social-positive dimensions of self-concept. We expected a negative and moderate association between these two constructs, in line with the argument that favourable and unfavourable views of the self can coexist. Moreover, we expected that positive social self-concept will be negatively associated with negative self-concept and positively associated with positive self-concept. However, these two associations are expected to vary in magnitude.

4.4 Methods

4.4.1 Participants

In this section, participants from Sample 1 ($N = 394$) (described earlier) were included in the analyses.

4.4.2 Measures

General and Social Self-Concept

At each burst, participants responded to items that were adapted from the Children's Perceived Competence Scale (Harter, 1982). Instead of the "structure alternative format" (Harter, 1982, p. 89) in which participants have to choose between two statements, students were presented with single descriptions of self-perceptions and asked to rate the degree of agreement for each, using a five-point Likert scale ranging from 1 ("Strongly disagree") to 5 ("Strongly agree"). Three items were used to assess social positive competence (e.g., "I feel accepted by the other kids in my class"), and three to assess positive self-concept (e.g., "I feel good about the way I act"). Three items were also used to assess negative self-concept (e.g., "There are lots of things about myself that I would change if I could"). Descriptive statistics are reported in Table 5.

4.4.3 Plan of Analysis

The analysis to compare the single-time longitudinal and the measurement burst designs consisted of three main steps. First, two types of scores were

Table 5 Descriptive statistics and reliability of the measures of self-concept by time

Measure	Single						Burst		
	T1-1	T1-2	T2-1	T2-2	T3-1	T3-2	T1	T2	T3
Positive General									
M (SD)	4.01 (.66)	3.96 (.78)	3.98 (.78)	4.00 (.77)	4.00 (.74)	4.01 (.87)	3.99 (.64)	3.99 (.71)	4.01 (.69)
α	.61	.74	.75	.73	.73	.73	.78	.84	.84
	[.53, .67]	[.69, .78]	[.71, .80]	[.68, .77]	[.68, .77]	[.68, .77]	[.75, .81]	[.81, .87]	[.81, .86]
Within-level ω							.74	.74	.73
Between-level ω							.75	.75	.68
Negative General									
M (SD)	2.43 (.96)	2.43 (1.00)	2.44 (1.03)	2.48 (1.03)	2.37 (.10)	2.42 (1.02)	2.43 (.87)	2.46 (.93)	2.39 (.94)
α	.60	.67	.70	.66	.66	.71	.76	.80	.83
	[.52, .66]	[.61, .72]	[.64, .75]	[.61, .72]	[.59, .71]	[.65, .76]	[.73, .79]	[.77, .83]	[.79, .85]
Within-level ω							.64	.70	.70
Between-level ω							.14	.73	.80
Social Positive									
M (SD)	3.90 (.89)	3.94 (.91)	3.95 (.87)	3.93 (.89)	4.00 (.87)	4.01 (.81)	3.92 (.84)	3.94 (.82)	4.00 (.81)
α	.83	.82	.85	.84	.88	.84	.90	.90	.90
	[.80, .86]	[.79, .85]	[.82, .88]	[.82, .87],	[.85, .90]	[.81, .87]	[.89, .91]	[.89, .91]	[.89, .91]
Within-level ω	.82						.82	.85	.86

estimated for each dimension. Each participant provided eighteen scores for each dimension as a result of answering the same three items in six assessments. Those scores were used to create two estimates. The first are single mean scores (single time), computed by averaging the three items within each assessment. The second are the combined mean scores for the measurement burst, which were computed by combining the scores from assessments 1 and 2 within each burst. Each of the scales showed adequate levels of reliability, with Cronbach's alphas ranging from .61 to .88 for the single mean scores and from .76 to .90 for the combined mean scores (see Table 5). Third, across-time Pearson bivariate correlations were estimated for each dimension. The correlation coefficients from the single-time and the measurement burst design were then compared by means of a statistical significance test, as suggested by Steiger (1980) (see Table 6).

4.5 Results

4.5.1 Descriptive Statistics

As displayed in Table 5, scores on the positive, negative, and social self-concept remained relatively stable across time. A series of General Linear Models (GLM) were conducted for each dimension of the self-concept separately in order to test the main within-subject effect of time (estimates adjusted using the Greenhouse–Geisser correction). The models included the means at each of the six assessment times. As revealed by these analyses, the main effect of time was not statistically significant for positive self-concept, $F(4.66, 1.83) = .62, p = .67$, $\eta p^2 = .002$), and for negative self-concept, $F(4.59, 180) = .56, p = .26, \eta p^2 = .003$. For the social positive dimension, the effect of time was statistically significant, $F(4.41, 1.73) = 2.83, p = .02, \eta p^2 = .01$. As suggested by a statistically significant contrast, the change was linear, $F(2.70, 1.39) = 6.81$, $p = .01, \eta p^2 = .02$, but small in magnitude, with a slight increase of positive social self-concept across time. A similar pattern was observed in the estimates of the measurement burst, as revealed by a series of within-subjects GLM's which included the means of the three bursts for each dimension. While the main effect of time was not found to be statistically significant for positive self-concept, $F(1.94, 7.65) = .34, p = .70, \eta p^2 = .001$, and negative self-concept, $F(1.95, 7.70) = .34, p = .15, \eta p^2 = .005$, it was found to be statistically significant for the social positive dimension, $F(1.87, 7.36) = 4.46, p = .014, \eta p^2 = .01$.

Within time, participants scored lower on the negative dimension when compared to the others. For instance, at T1-1 the mean on the positive self-concept was 4.01 ($SD = .66$), and on social self-concept 3.90 ($SD = .89$), whereas on the negative self-concept it was 2.43 ($SD = .96$). A MANOVA

Table 6 Comparison of correlation coefficients on measures of self-concept

Correlation Comparison	Z_{obs}	Pearson's r		R^2	
		Single	Burst	Single	Burst
Positive General Self-Worth					
T1-1/T2-1 versus T1/T2 Burst	−8.21	.50 [.42, .57]	.70 [.64, .75]	0.25	0.49
T1-2/T2-2 versus T1/T2 Burst	−2.76	.64 [58, .70]	.70 [.64, .75]	0.41	0.49
T2-1/T3-1 versus T2/T3 Burst	−5.62	.64 [58, .70]	.76 [.70, .80]	0.41	0.58
T2-2/T3-2 versus T2/T3 Burst	−6.39	.63 [.56, .68]	.76 [.70, .80]	0.40	0.58
Negative General Self-Worth					
T1-1/T2-1 versus T1/T2 Burst	−8.01	.50 [.43, .57]	.70 [.65, .75]	0.25	0.49
T1-2/T2-2 versus T1/T2 Burst	−3.09	.63 [.57, .68]	.70 [.65, .75]	0.40	0.49
T2-1/T3-1 versus T2/T3 Burst	−5.41	.66 [.60, .71]	.76 [.71,.80]	0.44	0.58
T2-2/T3-2 versus T2/T3 Burst	−7.47	.61 [.55, .67]	.76 [.71,.80]	0.37	0.58
Social Positive Self-Worth					
T1-1/T2-1 versus T1/T2 Burst	−5.52	.64 [.58, .70]	.75 [.70, .79]	0.41	0.56
T1-2/T2-2 versus T1/T2 Burst	−5.66	.64 [.58, .70]	.75 [.70, .79]	0.41	0.56
T2-1/T3-1 versus T2/T3 Burst	−5.50	.70 [.64, .75]	.79 [.75, .83]	0.49	0.62
T2-2/T3-2 versus T2/T3 Burst	−6.64	.68 [.62, .73]	.79 [.75, .83]	0.46	0.62

that included the three dimensions simultaneously revealed that the differences among those means were statistically significant, $F(1.43, 1.56) = 3.38, p < .001$, $\eta p^2 = .49$). A similar pattern was observed at all three times, as displayed in Table 5. We did not observe any salient differences when the means of the single time and the measurement burst were compared. This suggests that the use of the measurement burst design did not change the magnitude of the attributes reported by the participants. Additionally, when dispersion statistics such as the standard deviation, kurtosis, and skewness were examined, there were minimal differences between the burst and the single-time design. In other words, the magnitude, distribution, and shape of the dimensions was not affected by the use of the measurement burst design.

Regarding the associations between the dimensions of self-concept using the measurement burst design estimates, as expected, the correlation between the positive and negative dimensions was statistically significant ($p <. 05$) and moderate at each of the assessment times ($r_{T1} = -.54$ [95% CI: $-.61, -.46$], $r_{T2} = -.53$, [95% CI: $-.60, -.46$] and $r_{T3} = -.53$[95% CI: $-.60, -.46$]). Moreover, the social dimension showed differential associations with the positive and negative dimensions. Specifically, the positive association between the positive and social dimensions was stronger in magnitude ($r_{T1} = .58$ [95% CI: $.51, .64$], $r_{T2} = .64$ [95% CI: $.58, .70$], and $r_{T3} = -.65$ [95% CI: $-.70, -.59$]), than the negative association between the negative and social dimensions ($r_{T1} = -.38$ [95% CI: $-.46, -.29$], $r_{T2} = -.40$ [95% CI: $-.48, -.31$], and $r_{T3} = -.41$). All these correlation coefficients were observed to be statistically significant ($p < .05$).

4.5.2 Internal Consistency and Multilevel Reliability

Although both designs showed acceptable levels of reliability, the analyses revealed that the measurement burst design provided more reliable scales than the single-time design, as evidenced by higher Cronbach's alpha (see Table 5). In the case of the positive dimension, the alphas of the single time ranged from .61 to .75, whereas in the measurement burst design, the coefficients were .78, .84, and .84 at T1, T2, and T3 respectively. A similar pattern was observed on the negative dimension, with alphas that ranged from .60 to .71 in the single time and .76, .80, and .90 at T1, T2, and T3, respectively, with the measurement burst design. Similarly, the reliability coefficients of the social dimension scales were lower for the single-time design (range = .82–.88) than for the burst design (.90 at each of the times). In considering the multilevel reliability estimates for the three scales across the three times, we found that for general positive self-concept, the within-level ω ranged between .73 and .74 for general positive self-concept, while the between-level ω were found to be between .75 and .68. For negative self-concept, the within-level ω estimates ranged from .64 to .70 and from .14 and .80 for the between-level. Finally, the within-level ω estimates for social positive self-concept were between .82 and .86 and ranged from .81 to .88 for the between-level.

4.5.3 Correlation Comparisons

Next, we compared the correlation coefficients for each burst across time with those of the measurement bursts. Results from the correlation comparison tests broadly showed that the correlations from the measurement burst design were statistically and significantly stronger than those from the single-time design (see Table 6). The difference was especially salient at the first bursts within each time for the positive (e.g., positive T1-1 r_{single} = .50 vs. r_{burst} = .70) and negative dimensions (T1-1 r_{single} = .50 vs. r_{burst} = .70), while smaller, yet still statistically significant differences were observed for the social self-concept dimension. For instance, while the correlation between T1-1 and T2-1 was .64 for the single time, the correlation between the combined measures T1 and T2 was .75 for the measurement burst design. According to the Steiger (1980) correlation comparison test, the between-time correlation coefficients were stronger when the measurement burst design was employed than when the single-time design was used across the three dimensions, as evidenced by statistically significant differences ($p < .05$).

4.6 Summary

This section aimed to describe the stability of three dimensions of self-concept in a short time period by comparing a single-time and a measurement burst design. Our hypothesis posited that the use of measurement bursts would increase the reliability of the measures as well as produce stronger between-time stability across three time points when compared with a single-time design. Overall, our findings largely supported this prediction. Specifically, the reliability estimates indicated stronger levels of internal consistency and multilevel reliability estimates when the various dimensions of self-concept were estimated by combining information from two assessments. Additionally, statistically significant differences were observed when the between-time correlation coefficients from the two types of designs were compared, revealing higher levels of stability when the measurement burst was used. These findings support the use of burst measurement designs to assess self-concept by showing how the timing of measurements, such as when they are separated by shorter time periods, might reduce the variability associated with the changing nature of early adolescence. Although fluctuation on self-concept constitutes an attractive source of information and study for developmental researchers, the primary objective of our Element was to target more stable estimates.

Our results show that capturing higher levels of stability by combining information from two assessments can be advantageous for the study of self-concept in developmental research. Specifically, by reducing intraindividual variations, the estimates provide confidence to draw conclusions on other outcomes (e.g., peer exclusion, victimization; Morrow et al., 2019). Unambiguously, we observed that the combination of items separated by a week resulted in stronger correlations across time than did the use of a single measurement point. This result is in line with previous evidence regarding the high levels of stability on the domains of self-concept examined in the present section, in both long (Cole et al. 2001; Huang, 2010; Kruster & Orth, 2013) and short time periods (Hank & Baltes-Götz, 2019). Furthermore, it adds evidence to a field dominated by two extreme time poles (days versus years) with a design separated by one week. That said, measurement bursts can also be flexibly used to study intraindividual variations in self-concept. Given that daily fluctuations in adolescent reports of self-concept can occur (Nelis & Bukowski, 2019), the measurement burst design can provide additional information regarding why self-concept changes over the course of days, but also the ways in which it is generally stable across time. In doing so, researchers could further their understanding of the mechanisms that can influence one's self-concept from different temporal perspectives.

A secondary purpose of this section was to describe the multiple dimensions of self-concept. Specifically, we focused on distinguishing between the positive and negative general self-concept. Although previous theoretical models and empirical findings support the coexistence of favourable and unfavourable self-perceptions (Harter, 2006), the existing scoring procedures can make it difficult to examine the potential variations in terms of its valence. To address this, our measure asked participants to rate their agreement with single descriptions of the self-perceptions assessing positive and negative valences independently. In general, our findings seem to suggest that studying the self-concept beyond the positive valence provides important information with respect to its associations with other constructs. In addition to our findings about the coexistence of both a positive and a negative "side" of the self, this approach appeared to be useful for more accurately understanding each participant's rating of the items, which could be difficult when negative or bipolar statements are presented (Kamoen et al., 2013). Clearly, there are many interesting avenues for further research which includes the comparison between the alternative choice format and the single independent description and the degree to which individuals interpret the items in a similar manner. Moreover, further investigations that use the measurement burst within a longitudinal design should study the correlates and consequences of having a positive and a negative self-concept, as doing so can provide new insights into the extent to which these two selves differ.

4.7 Strengths, Limitations, and Future Directions

With regards to the observed associations between the three self-concept dimensions, the results are consistent with findings from longitudinal studies with measurement times separated by years (Cole et al. 2001; Huang, 2010; Kruster & Orth, 2013). Specifically, the three dimensions seem to be highly stable across the three waves of assessment. Although we anticipated higher variations between the assessments within each burst, the mean-level of the constructs did not reveal pronounced changes, questioning the adequacy of the one-week interval used in this study. An interesting avenue for further research is whether analyses focused on dispersion statistics, such as the standard deviation, could reveal the benefit of measurement bursts used in the present study. For instance, in the Nelis and Bukowski (2019) study, the sample of early adolescents were asked to report daily levels of self-esteem for four days. They found that adolescents who presented higher day-to-day fluctuations in their self-esteem also presented higher levels of internalizing problems, such as feelings of loneliness, stress, and hopelessness, among others. Thus, future studies should explore other temporal samplings for the use of measurement burst designs in self-concept to study the intraindividual and interindividual differences that exist. Finally, the present study opens the possibility to exploring interesting research questions such as the application of measurement burst designs on other domains of self-concept linked to peer interactions. For instance, beyond the influence of achievement experiences, individuals use peers as reference points of comparison to form an idea of their academic self-concept (Bukowski & Raufelder, 2018). Moreover, this subtype of the self-evaluation seems to fluctuate more at the beginning of high school (Cole et al., 2001). One noteworthy research question would be to explore the extent to which measurement burst designs would help researchers navigate those variations in an effort to improve the precision and reliability of their assessments, as demonstrated in this section.

Our results have important theoretical and practical implications. From a construct perspective, self-concept is typically seen as positively valenced, which can underestimate the fact that one's feelings about themselves can be negatively influenced. These findings support the work by other researchers (e. g., Bukowski & Raufelder, 2018) who contend that the self can be positively and negatively viewed. Specifically, the overlap between the positive and the negative general self-concept with the social self suggest that a two-factor approach can better represent one's self-perceptions and how they can be differentially correlated with related domains or other constructs. More broadly, our findings also provide support for the measurement burst approach by studying the stability of the self across three times. However, the intraindividual variability that exists as a result of youth experiencing different situations in their social worlds can cause fluctuations in their self-perceptions. Thus, the measurement burst design can be particularly useful in potentially charting these fluctuations over a period of time (e.g., a school year) in order to better understand the short- and long-term consequences associated with this variability. Using this design should help to strengthen one's findings, which could then be used to inform psychoeducation or intervention programs for youth who may present with significantly lower perceptions of themselves.

5 Discussion and Concluding Thoughts

The purpose of this Element was to provide evidence for the utility of measurement burst designs as a novel approach within peer research. It was based on the premise that developmentalists and peer researchers alike strive for the most precise and accurate observations in order to assess change and variability, which is a particular advantage of measurement bursts. In three studies, we compared the burst measurement design with the single-time designs that are standard practice for longitudinal research studies. Overall, our hypothesis that the measurement burst approach would provide stronger and more reliable estimates on each of the measures of peer acceptance, anxiety, and the self-concept was supported.

5.1 Measurement Burst Designs and Peer Research

Research in peer relationships studies a variety of social-emotional constructs. Sociometric assessments of acceptance and rejection within the peer group are standard within the peer literature (e.g., Cillessen & Bukowski, 2018; McDonald & Asher, 2018), but so are experiences with anxiety (e.g., La Greca & Harrison, 2005; La Greca & Lopez, 1998; Woodward & Fergusson, 2001) and perceptions of the self (e.g., Deković & Meeus, 1997; Preckel et al., 2013). Adolescence is a period of biological, cognitive, and social-emotional transitions and development. The changes that occur at the cognitive level, in particular, allow youth to be more capable of describing their feelings and experiences regarding anxiety (including other internalizing experiences) and the self-concept, including gains in abstract thinking and the ability to engage in greater social comparisons with their peers and potential worrying. While taking this into account, researchers should also ensure that the questionnaires they use are not only developmentally appropriate but also as reliable and precise as possible. Measurement burst designs allow for the latter to be evaluated in that they include repeated measurements of the same items that should show stronger reliability estimates when compared with measures obtained at a single time point.

In the sections on internalizing symptoms and the self-concept, we observed the Cronbach's alpha to be stronger at each of the times when the assessments were combined at each burst as compared to the individual measurement. Although the alpha coefficients across the measures under study demonstrated high consistency, they do not consider the hierarchical structure of the data. Thus, the multilevel ω coefficients were computed to demonstrate the preciseness that measurement bursts offer to the study of within-person and between-person variability. Using the two-level MCFA, our ω reliability estimates were generally higher than the Cronbach's alpha. In the case of negative general self-concept at Burst 1 where the coefficient was less than adequate, there was steady improvement at each of the subsequent bursts. Recall that alpha is biased as a function of sample size and does not account for individual change, especially if the same items are tested multiple times. With the multilevel approach within measurement bursts, peer researchers can be more confident in the reliability and accuracy of their scales. From there, this allowed us to move forward in comparing the correlations of the three times (T1, T2, T3) with the individual assessments at the first (i.e., T1-1 with T2-1, T2-1 with T3-1) and second bursts (i.e., T1-2 with T2-2, T2-2 with T3-2). In tandem with the stronger reliability estimates, we found that the correlation coefficients that were an aggregate of the two assessments for each burst produced stronger estimates as compared to the individual assessments. In an effort to produce strong effects for commonly studied constructs in peer research, it is apparent that the measurement burst approach is successful in accomplishing this goal.

It is evident that the measurement burst design can be flexibly applied to longitudinal research (Rush & Hofer, 2017; Sliwinski, 2008, 2011). The ability to intensively measure physical, cognitive, or social-emotional phenomena over a short period of time (e.g., days) and over the course of multiple longitudinal points affords developmental researchers several advantages. For example, using different collection methods (e.g., diaries, EMAs) allows for more closely collected observations to study intraindividual change. In addition, it allows researchers the opportunity to increase the precision and quality of their data by collecting their data in bursts so as to (a) decrease participant burden and (b) assess variability and stability of constructs that can vary within short time frames. For our purposes, we argue that our findings have demonstrated clear support for the latter advantage. Specifically, our research questions sought to provide increased clarity with the measures that we used and to ensure that the phenomena under study were being accurately reported. It is apparent that measurement burst designs can address the common limitation of cross-sectional and longitudinal designs with single-time assessment regarding participants reporting on their feelings and experiences retrospectively or in a particular moment of time. This "snapshot" may not entirely represent an individual's global experiences. For example, an adolescent who gave a score of 2 to one of their classmates on the Likert ratings of liking might be doing so because of a recent negative or bad experience with that person (e.g., the classmate teased them). In that particular moment, the adolescent may not necessarily like their peer. However, with a single-time longitudinal design, it is difficult to conclude whether that adolescent has a globally negative view of that peer. Measurement bursts allow peer researchers to ask the question, "*How much do you like ...*" for each person in a given reference group (e.g., classroom) multiple times in a short span of time. In our studies, this was done twice within seven days. As a result, we obtain two observations of the same item in order to more clearly demonstrate how much this adolescent likes this particular peer. If the peer consistently receives a score of 1 or 2 across bursts, then we can conclude that this adolescent does not like them very much. However, if the score is higher, then this intraindividual variability can suggest that situational factors might explain the difference in findings. Depending on the research question of interest, observations that result in stability or variability pose exciting avenues for future research in peer relations.

Although our thesis was not entirely empirically demonstrated, we argue that the measurement burst design also decreases our likelihood of participant burden. As we mentioned at the outset of this Element, along with the significant benefits to longitudinal designs are limitations that can be detrimental to developmental research. Those who engage in longitudinal research are aware of the extra care that is put into retaining participants. However, participants may choose to drop out from studies for a variety of reasons. They may have moved away or, more likely, they are not interested or no longer have the time to participate. Longitudinal research designs might entice developmental scientists to study phenomena in as many ways as possible, which could result in large batteries of self-reports and sociometric assessments for participants to complete. Participant burden should be a major concern in any research, but even more so in longitudinal research.

Another important factor to keep in mind, specifically for those who study children and adolescents, is their attention span. Sustained attention shows incremental increases from childhood to adolescence (Raffaelli et al., 2005), but few specific estimates are suggested. Even so, adolescents might have difficulty genuinely responding to items on questionnaires in a single one-hour sitting. Thus, from a design perspective, measurement bursts allow researchers to collect their data more effectively while also expecting as accurate responses as possible. Our program of research is made possible with the support from schools, their administrators, and the teachers. Given that schools and classroom schedules are highly regimented, we must communicate how much we are imposing on the classes. In order to minimize this, the measurement burst can break up a one-hour data collection into two thirty-minute sessions, which is far more manageable for the researchers, and in our experience, for the teachers as well. Even more, the fact that measurement bursts can allow for the assessment of different constructs across multiple data collections also places less of a burden on the participants themselves. Specifically, not all measures need to be asked at each burst. Instead, researchers could focus on those measures that would require a measurement burst and then counterbalance the rest of their measures to be used at a particular session. For example, sociometric assessments were one of the core measures in our study that used the measurement burst approach; however, we counterbalanced other measures in each of the assessments, such that friendship quality measures were included at only one of the two times across all three times, so as to reduce repetition and burden on the participants.

Taken together, our findings support our hypothesis that measurement burst designs are a useful asset in the study of peer relationships. Moreover, we were able to replicate these effects in two ways. Specifically, the findings that measurement burst estimates were stronger than single-time estimates were replicated in three distinct, yet common peer-related experiences during adolescence. Moreover, these findings were supported across multiple samples, further supporting our initial predictions. Clearly, the measurement burst design affords peer researchers the opportunity to be more precise in the constructs that they are studying, but it also allows for more meaningful longitudinal research to be conducted by studying change in different ways. Thus, there are multiple avenues for future studies to apply this research design to study change in the context of peer relationships.

5.2 Moving Forward

Developmental scientists are constantly finding novel ways to be innovative in their respective fields. Peer relations research has evolved significantly since its early days, but some methods, such as sociometric assessments, have endured and adapted well to statistical advances. The measurement burst design method is not necessarily a new way of collecting data; rather, it has only been applied to populations, such as adults and older populations (Rast et al., 2012; Röcke et al., 2011). Nevertheless, true multidisciplinary research should also consider research design and measurement approaches from other disciplines and domains of research in order to more accurately address their questions of interest. Indeed, we believe that measurements such as sociometric assessments will endure within the study of peers; however, we argue that one way to improve upon it is to find ways to assess these items repeatedly and over a short period of time to improve its reliability. Hence, measurement bursts appear to be well suited to accomplishing this task.

As we think ahead, the paths for future research are infinite. Measurement bursts allow for the study of both intraindividual and interindividual variability and change. Thus, depending on the design and questions of the researcher, measurement bursts can further capture change at different levels to enable a better understanding of the active processes associated with human development. Whereas our focus in this Element was on the stability of peer acceptance, anxiety, and the self-concept across three times, future studies would benefit from investigating how these experiences change within a span of days across the school year. Doing so could provide additional information on how peer experiences vary at different levels of timing. Social relationships and experiences are influential to development and well-being (Hinde, 1979), and positive and negative experiences from these relations, including those from one's peers, can affect a child's or adolescent's well-being. Cross-sectional daily diary studies on affect and social functioning show that adolescents who reported more internalizing symptoms also experienced more fluctuations in negative affect (Nelis & Bukowski, 2019). Moreover, lower levels of peer-perceived social functioning were associated with increased variability in self-esteem. Studies such as this and those from others who report similar findings related to self-concept and social functioning (e.g., Molloy et al., 2011) suggest the need for applying the measurement burst design in a longer time frame while employing intensive assessments. We should note that our samples are limited, such that we did not capture the entire school year. That said, we recommend future studies to spread the data collections and their associated bursts to better study the effects across an entire school year. In addition, it is still important to note that the information to be gained at these short bursts as well as from the longer intervals would provide greater insights into the dynamic experiences that youth have with their peers and how much of an effect they have on their lives.

We should also point out that another advantage of measurement burst designs is the fact that the intensive bursts are nested within each time. The datasets that we used for our studies have two observations at each of the three times, resulting in six total assessments. With this in mind, analyses should account for this complex and nested structure by taking advantage of more advanced statistical analyses, including multilevel modelling (e.g., Sliwinski, 2008 Sliwinski et al., 2009), growth curve modelling (e.g., heterogeneous variability growth model; see Nestler, 2020), and even multilevel structural equation modelling (e.g., Rush et al., 2019), above and beyond general linear modelling. Given that the focus of our analyses was on comparing the stabilities of peer-related constructs using a single-time assessment with those of the measurement burst design, we were limited in what statistical tests we could perform. That being said, future work that employs this design would be best served by employing more complex statistical modelling techniques so as to more fully capture the dynamics of peer experiences and other social relationships. For instance, multilevel models can account for intraindividual variability as well as nested data, in addition to having the ability to include additional predictors. The ability to model these data in more complex forms surpasses the limitations imposed by bivariate linear approaches, such as correlation coefficients. An interesting avenue for future research would be to examine the moderating role of peer network features on the stability of the constructs addressed in this Element, and whether measurement burst designs might offer a different perspective to the one offered by traditional longitudinal studies. For instance, the most popular peers within a classroom can set social norms that might influence processes of friendship formation and maintenance (Laninga-Wijnen et al., 2017; Rambaran et al., 2013).

5.2.1 Anticipating Challenges

It is important to note that although measurement burst designs offer significant advantages for developmental research, there are important challenges to consider. We note two main methodological and analytical challenges for peer researchers. First, the measurement burst is nested within longitudinal research; thus, it assumes many of the limitations that come with using this type of design. Issues such as the cost of conducting long-term studies are an inherent limitation to the use of measurement bursts. Moreover, we have suggested that the use of intensive assessments within each burst is advantageous because data collections can consist of measures that require the burst but also items that tap into other constructs. Nevertheless, participant retention remains a critical factor in any developmental research design, and measurement bursts are no exception (Stawski et al., 2016); clearly, extra efforts are needed to keep in touch with participants during the span of the entire study in order to keep them interested and involved. Additionally, questions about the construct when designing a study using this approach should consider the construct of interest and how it could vary within the short and long term. For example, we saw minimal change in the mean scores reported in peer acceptance, anxiety, and self-concept when the assessments were made one week apart. However, there might be increased variability if the assessments were more closely evaluated and intensive (e.g., within days). As such, there is a need to reflect on both the short-term and long-term needs for studying various constructs, given that they change at different times (Stawski et al., 2016). Indeed, it is important and necessary to carefully consider what is a reasonable and appropriate time frame both within the burst and over time in order to effectively study the construct of interest (Stawski et al., 2016). The conception and development of any research study will naturally be complicated and difficult; however, including measurement bursts within the longitudinal framework poses additional challenges. In the studies we discussed in this Element, we used what could be construed as a minimum number of assessments to be characterized as a measurement burst. That is, each burst had two assessments of data collection separated by one week. Our decision to do so was based on the need to work within the classroom schedules and as part of larger projects. Despite this limitation, we still argue that measurement bursts are a particularly novel approach to study change in peer status. Given that status as well as individual perceptions of anxiety and self-concept can vary on any given day due to a variety of factors (e.g., situations or events), a design where these are intensively studied daily within the measurement burst format would offer unique insights into the change that occurs within and across participants. For example, such a design could have participants respond on the degree to which they like their classmates and identify their top three friends daily for five consecutive days, across three different points during the school year. In doing so, researchers would be able to assess variability both within- and between-person in terms of how their liking scores vary within and across bursts. Taken further, they would then be able to examine the degree to which these scores and nominations vary as a function of time using growth curve modeling and also how they predict commonly studied peer behaviours (e.g., prosocial behaviour, aggression).

The second challenge is directly related to variables within peer research and their corresponding analytical options. Sociometric assessments afford peer researchers the opportunity to create not only profiles of youth within a given reference group but also a profile of the reference group itself. In this Element, we controlled for variations as a function of class size (see Velásquez et al., 2013) but not for status or structural characteristics. In studying changes to peer status within and across bursts, analyses will need to account for the extent to which there is change in status at the level of the reference group(s). For example, using classrooms as the reference group, stochastic actor-oriented models including SIENA (e.g., Steglich et al., 2010) that estimate peer-group level characteristics based on the relational ties among the group members can be especially useful in this regard. Characteristics such as classroom density (i.e., the number of friends a student nominates in their class) and reciprocity (i.e., mutual ties between classmates) are of particular importance to understand network influences on group dynamics (Veenstra et al., 2013). Moreover, the ability to incorporate multiple points from the measurement burst within a SIENA framework can provide new insights into how peer networks influence dynamics and variations in behaviour and vice versa. To our knowledge, this methodology has not been used in burst designs but represents new opportunities to further understand the dynamics of change within peer relationships.

5.3 Some Final Remarks

Measurement burst designs are highly adaptable and are not necessarily domain-specific. They are, however, sensitive to the research questions under consideration. Measurement burst designs might look differently for those who wish to study intraindividual versus interindividual change and variability. The focus of our research prioritized improving the stabilities for measures of peer acceptance, anxiety, and self-concept, which are commonly reported within the peer literature (e.g., Jiang & Cillessen, 2005). However, for those who wish to study intraindividual change, for example, the measurement burst design could look considerably different in its design and its method. Nevertheless, such a design that is both adaptable and manageable should give new ways to study concepts that are typically studied in a particular manner not only to peer relations researchers but also to others across a wide array of domains in psychology and abroad. In sum, strong and rigorous research methods continue to be a pillar for producing high-quality research. As such, measurement burst designs are a useful tool to help achieve this ever-important goal.

Appendix: Summary of Scales and Items

Scale	English	Spanish	Anchors
Sociometric – Liking Rating			
	How much do you like [name of participating classmate]?	¿Qué tanto te agrada [nombre compañeros participantes]?	1 = "Really do not like"; "No me agrada para nada" 2 = "Do not like"; "No me agrada" 3 = "Sort of like"; "Me agrada un poco" 4 = "Like"; Me agrada" 5 = "Like very much"; Me agrada mucho"
Sociometric Nominations			
	Who are your three best friends?	¿Quiénes son tus tres mejores amigos?	
Social Anxiety			
	I can feel nervous when I am with other kids in my class.	Puedo sentirme nervioso cuando estoy con otros niños de mi clase.	1 = "Never"; "Nunca" 2 = "Almost never"; "Casi nunca" 3 = "Sometimes"; "A veces" 4 = "Often"; "Muchas veces" 5 = "Almost always"; "Casi siempre"
	I worry about what other people might think of me.	Me preocupa lo que los demás pueden pensar de mí.	
	Sometimes I am afraid that some people in my class might make fun of me.	A veces me da miedo que los demás puedan burlarse de mí.	

Test Anxiety

I worry about not doing well in a test in school.

Me preocupa que no me vaya bien en un examen o prueba del colegio.

I get nervous before I have to take a test in class.

Me pongo nervioso antes de empezar un examen o prueba en clase.

After I take a test, I worry a lot about how I did on it.

Después de haber tomado un examen o prueba, me preocupo mucho por cómo me fue.

1 = "Never"; "Nunca"
2 = "Almost never"; "Casi nunca"
3 = "Sometimes"; "A veces"
4 = "Often"; "Muchas veces"
5 = "Almost always"; "Casi siempre"

Positive Self-Concept

I feel good about the way I act.

I am generally sure that what I am doing is right.

There are a lot of things about myself that I am proud of.

1 = "Never"
2 = "Almost never"
3 = "Sometimes"
4 = "Often"
5 = "Almost always"

(Continued)

(Continued)

Scale	English	Spanish	Anchors
Negative Self-Concept			
	There are lots of things about myself that I would change if I could.		1 = "Never"
			2 = "Almost never"
			3 = "Sometimes"
	I think that I am not a good person.		4 = "Often"
			5 = "Almost always"
	I do not like the way I do a lot of things.		
Positive Social Self-Concept			
	The other kids in the class like me.		1 = "Never"
			2 = "Almost never"
			3 = "Sometimes"
	Other kids in the class like me for who I am.		4 = "Often"
			5 = "Almost always"
	I feel accepted by the other kids in my class.		

References

Alessandri, G., Vecchione, M., Donnellan, B., & Tisak, J. (2013). An application of the LC-LSTM framework to the self-esteem instability case. *Psychometrika, 78*, 769–792. doi: 10.1007/S11336-013-9326-4

Almeida, D. M., McGonagle, K., & King, H. (2009). Assessing daily stress processes in social surveys by combining stressor exposure and salivary cortisol. *Biodemography and Social Biology, 55*(2), 219–237. doi: https://doi.org/10.1080/19485560903382338

Asher, S. R., & Dodge, K. A. (1986). Identifying children who are rejected by their peers. Developmental Psychology, 22(4), 444–449. https://doi.org/10.1037/0012-1649.22.4.444

Asher, S. R., Singleton, L. C., Tinsley, B. R., & Hymel, S. (1979). A reliable sociometric measure for preschool children. *Developmental Psychology, 15* (4), 443–444. doi: https://doi.org/10.1037/0012-1649.15.4.443

Baltes, P. B. (1987). Theoretical propositions of life-span developmental psychology: On the dynamics between growth and decline. *Developmental Psychology, 23*(5), 611–626. doi: 10.1037/0012-1649.23.5.611

Barlow, D. H., Ellard, K. K., Sauer-Zavala, S., Bullis, J. R., & Carl, J. R. (2014). The origins of neuroticism. *Perspectives on Psychological Science, 9*(5), 481–496. doi: 10.1177/1745691614544528

Berne, S., Frisén, A., Schultze-Krumbholz, A. et al. (2013). Cyberbullying assessment instruments: A systematic review. *Aggression and Violent Behavior, 18*(2), 320–334. doi: 10.1016/j.avb.2012.11.022

Blakemore, S. J., & Mills, K. L. (2014). Is adolescence a sensitive period for sociocultural processing? *Annual Review of Psychology, 65*, 187–207. doi: 10.1146/annurev-psych-010213-115202

Blume, F., Schmidt, A., Kramer, A. C., Schmiedke, F., & Neubauer, A. B. (2020, August 4). Homeschooling during the SARS-CoV-2 pandemic: The role of students' trait self-regulation and task attributes of daily learning tasks for students' daily self-regulation. doi: 10.31234/osf.io/tnrdj

Bonnet, D. G., & Wright, T. A. (2000). Sample size requirements for estimating Pearson, Kendall and Spearman correlations. *Psychometrica, 65*(1), 23–28. doi: 10.1007/BF02294183

Bosquet, M., & Egeland, B. (2006). The development and maintenance of anxiety symptoms from infancy through adolescence in a longitudinal sample. *Development and Psychopathology, 18*(2), 517–550. doi: 10.1017/S0954579406060275

Boulton, M. J., Smith, P. K., & Cowie, H. (2010). Short-term longitudinal relationships between children's peer victimization/bullying experiences and self-perceptions: Evidence for reciprocity. *School Psychology International*, *31*(3), 296–311. doi: 10.1177/0143034310362329

Broeren, S., & Muris, P. (2009). The relation between cognitive development and anxiety phenomena in children. *Journal of Child and Family Studies*, *18* (6), 702–709. doi: 10.1007/s10826-009-9276-8

Broeren, S., Muris, P., Diamantopoulou, S., & Baker, J. R. (2013). The course of childhood anxiety symptoms: Developmental trajectories and child-related factors in normal children. *Journal of Abnormal Child Psychology*, *41*(1), 81–95. doi: 10.1007/s10802-012-9669-9

Brown, B. B. (2004). Adolescents' relationships with peers. In R. M. Lerner & L. Steinberg (Eds.), *Handbook of adolescent psychology* (pp. 363–394). New York: John Wiley & Sons.

Brown, B. B., & Larson, J. (2009). Peer relationships in adolescents. In R. M. Lerner & L. Steinberg (Eds.), *Handbook of adolescent psychology* (pp. 74–103). New York: John Wiley & Sons.

Bukowski, W. M., Castellanos, M., & Persram, R. J. (2017). The current status of peer assessment techniques and sociometric methods. In P. E. L. Marks & A. H. N. Cillessen (Eds.), *New Directions in Peer Nomination Methodology. New Directions for Child and Adolescent Development*, *157*, 75–82. doi: 10 .1002/cad.20209

Bukowski, W. M., Castellanos, M., Vitaro, F., & Brendgen, M. (2015). Socialization and experiences with peers. In J. E. Grusec & P. D. Hastings (Eds.), *Handbook of socialization: Theory and research* (pp. 228–250). New York: Guilford.

Bukowski, W. M. , Cillessen, A. H. N., & Velasquez, A. M. (2012). The use of peer ratings in developmental research. In B. Laursen, T. Little, N. Card (Eds.), *Handbook of developmental research methods* (pp. 211–228). New York: Guilford.

Bukowski, W. M., & Hoza, B. (1989). Popularity and friendship: Issues in theory, measurement, and outcome. In T. J. Berndt & G. W. Ladd (Eds.), *Peer relationships in child development* (pp. 15–45). Oxford: UK: Wiley.

Bukowski, W. M., Laursen, B., & Rubin, K. H. (2018). Peer relations: Past, present, and promise. In W. M. Bukowski, B. Laursen, & K. H. Rubin (Eds.), *Handbook of peer interactions, relationships, and groups* (pp. 3–20). New York: Guilford.

Bukowski, W. M., & Newcomb, A. F. (1984). Stability and determinants of sociometric status and friendship choice: A longitudinal perspective. *Developmental Psychology*, *20*(5), 941–952. doi: 10.1037/0012-1649.20.5.941

References 69

Bukowski, W. M., & Raufelder, D. (2018). Peers and the self. In W. M. Bukowski, B. Laursen, & K. H. Rubin (Eds.), *Handbook of peer interactions, relationships, and groups* (pp. 141–156). New York: Guilford.

Bukowski, W. M., Sippola, L., Hoza, B., & Newcomb, A. F. (2000). Pages from a sociometric notebook: An analysis of nomination and rating scale measures of acceptance, rejection, and social preference. *New Directions for Child and Adolescent Development*, 2000(88), 11–26.

Byrne, B. M. (1996). *Measuring self-concept across the life span: Issues and instrumentation*. Washington, DC: American Psychological Association. doi: 10.1037/10197-000

Carleton, R. N. (2016). Into the unknown: A review and synthesis of contemporary models involving uncertainty. *Journal of Anxiety Disorders*, *39*, 30–43. doi: 10.1016/j.janxdis.2016.02.007

Carmines, E. G., & Zeller, R. A. (1979). *Reliability and validity assessment*. Newbury Park, CA: Sage.

Chapin, F. S. (1920). *Field work and social research*. New York, The Century Company.

Cho, G., Pasquini, G., & Scott, S. B. (2019). Measurement burst designs in lifespan developmental research. In R. Knight, S. D. Neupert, N. D. Anderson, H. W. Wahl, & N. A. Pachana (Eds.), *Oxford Research Encyclopedia of Psychology* (pp. 1–28). Oxford University Press USA. doi: https://doi.org/10.1093/acrefore/9780190236557.013.348

Cillessen, A. H. N. (2008). Sociometric methods. In K. H. Rubin, W. M. Bukowski, & B. Laursen (Eds.), *Handbook of peer interactions, relationships, and groups* (pp. 82–99). New York: Guilford.

Cillessen, A. H. N., & Borch, C. (2006). Developmental trajectories of adolescent popularity: A growth curve modelling analysis. *Journal of Adolescence*, *29*(6), 935–959. doi: 10.1016/j.adolescence.2006.05.005

Cillessen, A. H. N., & Bukowski, W. M. (2018). Sociometric perspectives. In W. M. Bukowski, B. Laursen, & K. H. Rubin (Eds.), *Handbook of peer interactions, relationships, and groups* (pp. 64–83). New York: Guilford.

Cillessen, A. H. N., & Marks, P. E. L. (2011). Conceptualizing and measuring popularity. In A. H. N. Cillessen, D. Schwartz, & L. Mayeux (Eds.), *Popularity in the peer system* (pp. 25–56). New York: Guilford.

Cillessen, A. H. N., & Marks, P. E. L. (2017). Methodological choices in peer nomination research. In P. E. L. Marks & A. H. N. Cillessen (Eds.), *New Directions in Peer Nomination Methodology. New Directions for Child and Adolescent Development*, *157*, 21–44. doi: 10.1002/cad.20206

Cillessen, A. H., & Mayeux, L. (2004). From censure to reinforcement: Developmental changes in the association between aggression and social status. *Child Development*, *75*(1), 147–163. doi: 10.1111/j.1467-8624.2004.00660.x

Cillessen, A. H. N., Schwartz, D., & Mayeux, L. (2011). Preface. In *Popularity in the peer system* (pp. ix–xii). New York: Guilford.

Cillessen, A. H. N., & van den Berg, Y. H. M. (2012). Popularity and school adjustment. In A. Ryan & G. W. Ladd (Eds.), *Peer relationships and adjustment at school* (pp. 135–164). Charlotte, NC: Information Age Publishing.

Coie, J. D., Dodge, K. A., & Coppotelli, H. (1982). Dimensions and types of social status: A cross-age perspective. *Developmental Psychology*, *18*(4), 557–570. doi: https://doi.org/10.1037/0012-1649.18.4.557

Cole, D. A., Maxwell, S. E., Martin, J. M. et al.(2001). The development of multiple domains of child and adolescent self- concept: A cohort sequential longitudinal design. *Child Development*, *72*(6), 1723–1746. doi: https://doi.org/10.1111/1467-8624.00375

Criss, M. M., Pettit, G. S., Bates, J. E., Dodge, K. A., & Lapp, A. L. (2002). Family adversity, positive peer relationships, and children's externalizing behaviour: A longitudinal perspective on risk and resilience. *Child Development*, *73*(4), 1220–1237. doi: https://doi.org/10.1111/1467-8624.00468

Cronbach, L. J. (1951). Coefficient alpha and the internal structure of tests. *Psychometrika*, *16*(1951), 297–334. doi: https://doi.org/10.1007/BF02310555

Danneel, S., Geukens, F., Maes, M. et al. (2020). Loneliness, social anxiety symptoms, and depressive symptoms in adolescence: Longitudinal distinctiveness and correlated change. *Journal of Youth and Adolescence*, *49*(11), 2246–2264. doi: https://doi.org/10.1007/s10964-020-01315-w

de Bruyn, E. H., Cillessen, A. H. N., & Wissink, I. B. (2010). Associations of peer acceptance and perceived popularity with bullying and victimization in early adolescence. *Journal of Early Adolescence*, *30*(4), 543–566. doi: https://doi.org/10.1177/0272431609340517

Deković, M., & Meeus, W. (1997). Peer relations in adolescence: Effects of parent and adolescents' self-concept. *Journal of Adolescence*, *20*(2), 163–176. doi: https://doi.org/10.1006/jado.1996.0074

Dodge, K. A., Bates, J. E., & Pettit, G. S. (1990). Mechanisms in the cycle of violence. *Science*, *250*(4988), 1678–1683. doi: https://doi.org/10.1126/science.2270481

Eisenberg, N., Guthrie, I. K., Murphy, B. C. et al. (1999). Consistency and development of prosocial dispositions: A longitudinal study. *Child Development*, *70*(6), 1360–1372. doi: https://doi.org/10.1111/1467-8624.00100

Festinger, L. (1954). A theory of social comparison processes. *Human Relations*, *7*(2), 117–140. doi: https://doi.org/10.1177/001872675400700202

Fialko, L., Bolton, D., & Perrin, S. (2012). Applicability of a cognitive model of worry to children and adolescents. *Behaviour Research and Therapy, 50*(5), 341–349. doi: https://doi.org/10.1016/j.brat.2012.02.003

Field, A. P., & Lester, K. J. (2010). Learning of information processing biases in anxious children and adolescents. In J. A. Hadwin & A. P. Field (Eds.), *Information processing biases and anxiety: A developmental perspective* (pp. 253–278). Wiley. Blackwell. doi: https://doi.org/10.1002/9780470661468.ch11

Fiske, D. W., & Rice, L. (1955). Intra-individual response variability. *Psychological Bulletin, 52*(3), 217–250. doi: https://doi.org/10.1037/h0045276

Fortes, M., Delignières, D., & Ninot, G. (2004). The dynamics of self-esteem and physical self: Between preservation and adaptation. *Quality & Quantity: International Journal of Methodology, 38*(6), 735–751. doi: https://doi.org /10.1007/s11135-004-4764-9

Geiser, C., Keller, B. T., Lockhart, G. et al. (2015). Distinguishing state variability from trait change in longitudinal data: The role of measurement (non) invariance in latent state-trait analyses. *Behavior Research Methods, 47*(1), 172–203. doi: https://doi.org/10.3758/s13428-014-0457-z.

Geldhof, G. J., Preacher, K. J., & Zyphur, M. J. (2014). Reliability estimation in a multilevel confirmatory factor analysis framework. *Psychological Methods, 19*(1), 72–91. doi: https://doi.org//10.1037/a0032138

Gentile, D. A., Choo, H., Liau, A. et al. (2011). Pathological video game use among youths: A two-year longitudinal study. *Pediatrics, 127*(2), e319–e329. doi: https://doi.org/10.1542/peds.2010-1353

Gest, S. D., Domitrovich, C. E., & Welsh, J. A. (2005). Peer academic reputation in elementary school: Associations with changes in self-concept and academic skills. *Journal of Educational Psychology, 97*(3), 337–346. doi: https://doi.org/10.1037/0022-0663.97.3.337

Gullone, E. (2000). The development of normal fear: A century of research. *Clinical Psychology Review, 20*(4), 429–451. doi: https://doi.org/10.1016 /S0272-7358(99)00034-3

Gullone, E., King, N. J., & Ollendick, T. H. (2001). Self-reported anxiety in children and adolescents: A three-year follow-up study. *The Journal of Genetic Psychology, 162*(1), 5–19. doi: https://doi.org/10.1080 /00221320109597878

Gustavson, K., von Soest, T., Karevold, E., & Røysamb, E. (2012). Attrition and generalizability in longitudinal studies: Findings from a 15-year population-based study and a Monte Carlo simulation study. *BMC Public Heatlh, 12*(918), 1–11. doi: https://doi.org/10.1186/1471-2458-12-918

Hank, P., & Baltes-Götz, B. (2019). The stability of self-esteem variability: A real-time assessment. *Journal of Research in Personality*, *79* (April), 143–150 doi: https://doi.org/10.1016/j.jrp.2019.03.004

Harris, M. A., & Orth, U. (2020). The link between self-esteem and social relationships: A meta-analysis of longitudinal studies. *Journal of Personality and Social Psychology*, 119(6), 1459–1477. doi: https://doi.org/10.1037/pspp0000265

Harter, S. (1982). The perceived competence scale for children. *Child Development*, *53*(1), 87–97. doi: https://doi.org/10.2307/1129640

Harter, S. (2012) *Self-perception profile for adolescents: Manual and questionnaires*. 2012 Revision. Denver, CO: University of Denver. doi: https://portfolio.du.edu/SusanHarter/page/44210

Harter, S. (2006). The Self. In N. Eisenberg, W. Damon, & R. M. Lerner (Eds.), *Handbook of child psychology: Social, emotional, and personality development* (pp. 505–570). Wiley.

Harter, S. (2012). *The construction of the self: Developmental and sociocultural foundations* (2nd ed.). New York: Guilford.

Harter, S. (1988). Self-perception profile for adolescents: Manual and questionnaires. Denver, CO: University of Denver. https://portfolio.du.edu/SusanHarter/page/44210

Harter, S. (1985). Self-perception profile for children: Manual and questionnaires. Denver, CO: University of Denver. https://portfolio.du.edu/SusanHarter/page/44210

Hearn, C. S., Donovan, C. L., Spence, S. H., March, S., & Holmes, M. C. (2017). What's the worry with social anxiety? Comparing cognitive processes in children with generalized anxiety disorder and social anxiety disorder. *Child Psychiatry & Human Development*, *48*(5), 786–795. doi: https://doi.org/10.1007/s10578-016-0703-y.

Hinde, R. A. (1979). *Towards understanding relationships*. London: Academic Press.

Holfield, B., & Leadbeater, B. J. (2017). Concurrent and longitudinal associations between early adolescents' experiences of school climate and cyber victimization. *Computers in Human Behaviour*, *76*, 321–328. doi: https://doi.org/10.1016/j.chb.2017.07.037

Hong, R. Y., Lee, S. S., Tsai, F. F., & Tan, S. H. (2017). Developmental trajectories and origins of a core cognitive vulnerability to internalizing symptoms in middle childhood. *Clinical Psychological Science*, *5*(2), 299–315. doi: https://doi.org/10.1177/2167702616679875

Howe, N., Ross, H. S., & Recchia, H. (2011). Sibling relations in early and middle childhood. In P. K. Smith & C. H. Hart (Eds.), *The Wiley-Blackwell handbook of childhood social development* (2nd ed., pp. 356–372). Hoboken, NJ: Wiley-Blackwell.

Huang, C. (2010). Mean-level change in self-esteem from childhood through adulthood: Meta-analysis of longitudinal studies. *Review of General Psychology, 14*(3), 251–260. doi: https://doi.org/10.1037/a0020543

Hymel, S., Rubin, K. H., Rowden, R., & LeMare, L. (1990). Children's peer relationships: Longitudinal prediction of internalizing and externalizing problems from middle to late childhood. *Child Development, 61*(6), 2004–2021. doi: https://doi.org/10.2307/1130854

Jiang, X. L., & Cillessen, A. H. N. (2005). Stability of continuous measures of sociometric status: A meta-analysis. *Developmental Review, 25*(1), 1–25. doi: https://doi.org/10.1016/j.dr.2004.08.008

Kamoen, N., Holleman, B., van den Bergh, H., & Sanders, T. (2013). Positive, negative, and bipolar questions: The effect of question polarity on ratings of text readability. *Survey Research Methods, 7*(3), 181–189. doi: https://doi.org /10.18148/srm/2013.v7i3.5034

Karlson, C. W., & Rapoff, M. A. (2009). Attrition in randomized controlled trials for pediatric chronic conditions. *Journal of Pediatric Psychology, 34* (7), 782–793. doi: https://doi.org/10.1093/jpepsy/jsn122

Kerns, C. M., Read, K. L., Klugman, J., & Kendall, P. C. (2013). Cognitive behavioral therapy for youth with social anxiety: Differential short and long-term treatment outcomes. *Journal of Anxiety Disorders, 27*(2), 210–215. doi: https://doi.org/10.1016/j.janxdis.2013.01.009

Kingery, J. N., Erdley, C. A., & Marshall, K. C. (2011). Peer acceptance and friendship as predictors of early adolescents' adjustment across the middle school transition. *Merill-Palmer Quarterly, 57*(3), 215–243. doi: https://doi .org/10.1353/mpq.2011.0012

Klima, T., & Repetti, R. L. (2008). Children's peer relations and their psycho-logical adjustment: Differences between close friendships and the larger peer group. *Merrill-Palmer Quarterly, 54*(2), 151–178. doi: https://doi.org/10 .1353/mpq.2008.0016

Kuster, F., & Orth, U. (2013). The long-term stability of self-esteem: Its time-dependent decay and nonzero asymptote. *Personality and Social Psychology Bulletin, 39*(5), 677-690. https://doi.org/10.1177 /0146167213480189

LaFontana, K. M., & Cillessen, A. H. (2010). Developmental changes in the priority of perceived status in childhood and adolescence. *Social Development, 19*(1), 130–147. doi: https://doi.org/10.1111/j.1467-9507.2008.00522.x

La Greca, A. M., & Harrison, H. M. (2005). Adolescent peer relations, friend-ships, and romantic relationships: Do they predict social anxiety and depression? *Journal of Clinical Child and Adolescent Psychology, 34*(1), 49–61. doi: https://doi.org/10.1207/s15374424jccp3401_5

La Greca, A. M., & Lopez, N. (1998). Social anxiety among adolescents: Linkages with peer relations and friendships. *Journal of Abnormal Child Psychology, 26*(2), 83–94. doi: https://doi.org/10.1023/A: 1022684520514

Laninga-Wijnen, L., Harakeh, Z., Steglich, C., et al. (2017). The norms of popular peers moderate friendship dynamics of adolescent aggression. *Child Development, 88*(4), 1265–1283. https://doi.org/10.1111/cdev.12650

Laninga-Wijnen, L., Ryan, A. M., Harakeh, Z., Shin, H., & Vollebergh, W. A. M. (2018). The moderating role of popular peers' achievement goals in 5th- and 6th-graders' achievement-related friendships: A social network analysis. *Journal of Educational Psychology, 110*(2), 289–307. doi: https://doi.org/lib-ezproxy.concordia.ca/10.1037/edu0000210

Laursen, B., & Bukowski, W. M. (1997). A developmental guide to the organisation of close relationships. *International Journal of Behavioural Development, 21*(4), 747–770. doi: https://doi.org//10.1080/016502597384659

Laursen, B., Bukowski, W. M., Nurmi, E., & Aunola, K. (2007). Friendship moderates prospective associations between social isolation and adjustment problems in young children. *Child Development, 78*(4), 1395–1404. doi: https://doi.org/10.1111/j.1467-8624.2007.01072.x

Lee, S., Koffer, R. E., Sprague, B. N. et al. (2018). Activity diversity and its associations with psychological well-being across adulthood. *The Journals of Gerontology Series B: Psychological Sciences and Social Sciences, 73*(6), 985–995. doi: https://doi.org/10.1093/geronb/gbw118

Lehman, B. J., & Repetti, R. L. (2007). Bad days don't end when the school bell rings: The lingering effects of negative school events on children's mood, self-esteem, and perceptions of parent-child interaction. *Social Development, 16*(3), 1–23. doi: https://doi.org/10.1111/j.1467-9507.2007.00398.x

Liao, Y., Chou, C-P. , Huh, J., Leventhal, A., & Dunton, G. (2017). Examining acute bidirectional relationships between affect, physical feeling states, and physical activity in free-living situations using electronic momentary assessment. *Journal of Behavioural Medicine, 40*(3), 445–457. doi: https:// doi.org/10.1007/s10865-016-9808-9

Lindzey, G. & Borgatta, E. F. (1954). Sociometric measurement. In *Handbook of Social Psychology* (pp. 405–448). Cambridge: Addison-Wesley Publishers Co.

Lingler, J. H., Schmidt, K. L., Gentry, A. L., Hu, L., & Terhorst, L. A. (2014). A new measure of research participant burden: Brief report. *Journal of Empirical Research on Human Research Ethics, 9*(4), 46–49. doi: https://doi .org/10.1177/1556264614545037

Luengo Kanacri, B. P., Eisenberg, N., & Thartori, E. et al. (2017). Longitudinal relations among positivity, perceived positive school climate, and prosocial behaviour in Colombian Adolescents. *Child Development*, *88*(4), 1100–1114. doi: https://doi.org/10.1111/cdev.12863

March, J. S. (2013). *Multidimensional Anxiety Scale for Children* (2nd ed.). Toronto: Multi-Health Systems.

Marks, P. E. L. (2017). Introduction to the special issue: 20th-century origins and 21st-century developments of peer nomination methodology. In P. E. L. Marks & A. H. N. Cillessen (Eds.), *New Directions in Peer Nomination Methodology. New Directions for Child and Adolescent Development*, 2017(157), 7–19. doi: https://doi.org/10.1002/cad.20205

Marshall, S. L., Parker, P. D., Ciarrochi, J., & Heaven, P. C. L. (2014). Is self-esteem a cause or consequence of social support? A 4-year longitudinal study. *Child Development*, *85*(3), 1275–1291. doi: https://doi.org/10.1111/cdev.12176

McDonald, K. L., & Asher, S. R. (2018). Peer acceptance, peer rejection, and popularity: Social-cognitive and behavioural perspectives. In W. M. Bukowski, B. Laursen, & K. H. Rubin (Eds.), *Handbook of peer interactions, relationships, and groups* (pp. 429–446). New York: Guilford.

McDonald, R. P. (1999). *Test theory: A unified treatment*. Lawrence Erlbaum.

McEvoy, P. M., & Mahoney, A. E. (2012). To be sure, to be sure: Intolerance of uncertainty mediates symptoms of various anxiety disorders and depression. *Behavior Therapy*, *43*(3), 533–545. doi: https://doi.org/10.1016/j.beth.2011.02.007

Molloy, L. E., Ram, N., & Gest, S. D. (2011). The storm and stress (or calm) of early adolescent self-concepts: Within- and between-subjects variability. *Developmental Psychology*, *47*(6), 1589–1607. doi: https://doi.org/10.1037/a0025413

Monroe, W. S. (1898). Discussion and reports. Social consciousness in children. *Psychological Review*, *5*(1), 68–70. doi: https://doi.org/10.1037/h0075859

Morrow, M. T., Hubbard, J. A., & Sharp, M. K. (2019). Preadolescents' daily peer victimization and perceived social competence: Moderating effects of classroom aggression. *Journal of Clinical Child & Adolescent Psychology*, *48*(5), 716–727. doi: https://doi.org/10.1080/15374416.2017.1416618

Muris, P., Vermeer, E., & Horselenberg, R. (2008). Cognitive development and the interpretation of anxiety-related physical symptoms in 4–13-year-old non-clinical children. *Journal of Behavior Therapy and Experimental Psychiatry*, *39*(1), 73–86. doi: https://doi.org/10.1016/j.jbtep.2006.10.014

Muthén, L. K., & Muthén, B. O. (2010). *Mplus User's Guide* (6th ed.). Los Angeles: Muthén & Muthén.

Nelemans, S. A., Hale, W. W., Branje, S. J., Meeus, W. H., & Rudolph, K. D. (2017). Individual differences in anxiety trajectories from Grades 2 to 8: Impact of the middle school transition. *Development and Psychopathology*, *30*(4), 1–15. doi: https://doi.org/10.1017/S0954579417001584

Nelemans, S. A., Hale, W. W., Branje, S. J. T. et al. (2014). Heterogeneity in development of adolescent anxiety disorder symptoms in an 8-year longitudinal community study. *Development and Psychopathology*, *26*(1), 181–202. https://doi.org/10.1017/S0954579413000503

Nelis, S., & Bukowski, W. M. (2019). Daily affect and self-esteem in early adolescence: Correlates of mean levels and within-person variability. *Psychologica Belgica*, *59*(1), 96–115. doi: https://doi.org/10.5334/pb.467

Nesselroade, J. R. (1990). The warp and woof of the developmental fabric. In R. Downs, L. Liben, & D. S. Palermo (Eds.), *Visions of aesthetics, the environment, and development: The legacy of Joachim F. Wohwill* (pp. 213–240). Mahwah, NJ: Lawrence Erlbaum Associates.

Nestler, S. (2020). Modeling intraindividual variability in growth with measurement burst designs. *Structural Equation Modeling: A Multidisciplinary Journal*, *28*(1), 28–39. doi: https://doi.org/10.1080/10705511.2020.1757455

Newcomb, A. F., & Bukowski, W. M. (1983). Social impact and social preferences as determinants of children's peer group status. *Developmental Psychology*, *19*(6), 856–867. doi: https://doi.org/10.1037/0012-1649.19.6.856

Newcomb, A. F., Bukowski, W. M., & Pattee, L. (1993). Children's peer relations: A meta-analytic review of popular, rejected, neglected, controversial, and average sociometric status. *Psychological Bulletin*, *113*(1), 99–128. doi: https://doi.org/10.1037/0033-2909.113.1.99

Nezlek, J. B. (2017). A practical guide to understanding reliability in studies of within-person variability. *Journal of Research in Personality*, *69*, 149–155. doi: https://10.1016/j.jrp.2016.06.020

Orth, U., & Robins, R. W. (2014) The development of self-esteem. *Current Directions in Psychological Science*, *23*(5), 381–387. doi: https://doi.org/10.1177/0963721414547414

Orth, U., Robins, R. W., & Widaman, K. F. (2012). Life-span development of self-esteem and its effects on important life outcomes. *Journal of Personality and Social Psychology*, *102*(6), 1271–1288. doi: https://doi.org/10.1037/a0025558

Owens, T. J. (1993) Accentuate the positive and the negative: Rethinking the use of self-esteem, self-deprecation, and self-confidence. *Social Psychology Quarterly*, *56*(4), 288–299. doi: https://doi.org/10.2307/2786665

Parker, J. G., Rubin, K. H., Erath, S. A., Wojslawowicz, J. C., & Burskirk, A. A (2006). Peer relationships, child development, and adjustment A developmental psychopathological perspective. In D. Cicchetti &

D. J. Cohen (Eds.), *Developmental psychopathology: Theory and method* (pp. 419–493). Hoboken, NJ: Wiley.

Parkhurst, J. T., & Hopmeyer, A. (1998). Sociometric popularity and peer-perceived popularity: Two distinct dimensions of peer status. *Journal of Early Adolescence*, *18*(2), 125–144. doi: https://doi.org/10.1177/0272431698018002001

Persram, R. J., Schwartzman, E., & Bukowski, W. M. (2021). The concurrent association between friendship security and friendship satisfaction is moderated by experience within the family context. *Merrill-Palmer Quarterly*, 67 (1), 56–75. doi: https://doi.org/10.13110/merrpalmquar1982.67.1.0056

Pettit, G. S., Laird, R. D., Dodge, K. A., Bates, J. E., & Criss, M. M. (2001). Antecedents and behaviour-problem outcomes of parental monitoring and psychological control in early adolescence. *Child Development*, *72*(2), 583–598. doi: https://doi.org/10.1111/1467-8624.00298

Poulin, F. & Chan, A. (2010). Friendship stability and change in childhood and adolescence. *Developmental Review*, *30*(3), 257–272. doi: https://doi.org/10 .1016/j.dr.2009.01.001

Preckel, F., Niepel, C., Schneider, M., & Brunner, M. (2013). Self-concept in adolescence: A longitudinal study on reciprocal effects of self-perceptions in academic and social domains. *Journal of Adolescence*, *36*(6), 1165–1175. doi: https://doi.org/10.1016/j.adolescence.2013.09.001

Prinstein, M. J. (2007). Moderators of peer contagion: A longitudinal examination of depression socialization between adolescents and their best friends. *Journal of Clinical Child and Adolescent Psychology*, *36*(2), 159–170. doi: https://doi.org/10.1080/15374410701274934

Prinstein, M. J., Borelli, J. L., Cheah, C. S. L., Simon, V. A., & Aikins, J. W. (2005). Adolescent girls' interpersonal vulnerability to depressive symptoms: A longitudinal examination of reassurance-seeking and peer relationships. *Journal of Abnormal Psychology*, *114*(4), 676–688. doi: https://doi.org /10.1037/0021-843X.114.4.676

Raffaelli, M., Crockett, L. J., & Shen, Y-L. (2005). Developmental stability and change in self-regulation from childhood to adolescence. *Journal of Genetic Psychology*, *166*(1), 54–76. doi: https://doi.org/10.3200/GNTP.166.1.54-76

Rambaran, A. J., Dijkstra, J. K., & Stark, T. H. (2013). Status-based influence processes: The role of norm salience in contagion of adolescent risk attitudes. *Journal of Research on Adolescence*, *23*(3), 574–585.

Rast, P., MacDonald, S. W. S., & Hofer, S. M. (2012). Intensive measurement designs for research on aging. *GeroPsych*, *25*(2), 45–55. doi: https://doi.org /10.1024/1662-9647/a000054

Renk, K., & Phares, V. (2004). Cross-informant ratings of social competence in children and adolescents. *Clinical Psychology Review, 24*(2), 239–254. doi: https://doi.org/10.1016/j.cpr.2004.01.004

Riediger, M., & Rauers, A. (2018). Experience sampling in lifespan developmental methodology. In *Oxford Research Encyclopedia of Psychology.* Oxford University Press. doi: https://doi.org/10.1093/acrefore/9780190236557.013.346

Röcke, C., Hoppmann, C. A., & Klumb, P. L. (2011). Correspondence between retrospective and momentary ratings of positive and negative affect in old age: Findings from a one-year measurement burst design. *The Journals of Gerontology Series B: Psychological Sciences and Social Sciences, 66B*(4), 411–415. doi: https://doi.org/10.1093/geronb/gbr024

Rubin, K. H., Booth, L., & Wilkinson, M. (1990). The Waterloo longitudinal project: Correlates and consequences of social withdrawal in childhood. *Infancia y Aprendizaje, 13*(49), 131–144. doi: https://doi.org/10.1080/02103702.1990.10822262

Rubin, K. H., Bukowski, W. M., & Parker, J. G. (2006). Peer interactions, relationships, and groups. In N. Eisenberg, W. Damon, & R. M. Lerner (Eds.), *Handbook of child psychology: Social, emotional, and personality development* (pp. 571–645). Hoboken, NJ: Wiley.

Rush, J., & Hofer, S. M. (2017). V. Design-based approaches for improving measurement in developmental science. *Developmental Methodology* (Vol. 82). Monographs of the Society for Research in Child Development, *82*(2), 67–83. doi: https://doi.org/10.1111/mono.12299

Rush, J., Rast, P., Almeida, D. M., & Hofer, S. M. (2019). Modeling long-term changes in daily within- person associations: An application of multilevel SEM. *Psychology and Aging, 34*(2), 163–176. doi: https://doi.org/10.1037/pag0000331

Schmidt, A., Neubauer, A. B., Dirk, J., & Schmiedek, F. (2020). The bright and the dark side of peer relationships: Differential effects of relatedness satisfaction and frustration at school on affective well-being in children's daily lives. *Developmental Psychology, 56*(8), 1532–1546. doi: https://doi.org/10.1037.dev0000997

Scott, S. B., Graham-Engeland, J. E., Engeland, C. G. et al. (2015). The effects of stress on cognitive aging, physiology, and emotion (ESCAPE) project. *BMC Psychiatry, 15*(146) 1–14. doi: https://doi.org/10.1186/s12888-015-0497-7

Sentse, M., Prinzie, P., & Salmivalli, C. (2017). Testing the direction of longitudinal paths between victimization, peer rejection, and different types of internalizing problems in adolescence. *Journal of Abnormal Child Psychology, 45*, 1013–1023. doi: https://doi.org/10.1007/s10802-016-0216-y

Setoh, P., Qin, L., Zhang, X., & Pomerantz, E. M. (2015). The social self in early adolescence: Two longitudinal investigations in the United States and China. *Developmental Psychology*, *51*(7), 949–961. doi: https://doi.org/10.1037/a0039354

Sharpe, L. M., & Frankel, J. (1983). Respondent burden: A test of some common assumptions. *Public Opinion Quarterly*, *47*(1), 36–53. doi: https://doi.org/10.1086/268765

Silver, R. B., Measelle, J. R., Armstrong, J. M., & Essex, M. J. (2010). The impact of parents, child care providers, teachers, and peers on early externalizing trajectories. *Journal of School Psychology*, *48*(6), 555–583. doi: https://doi.org/10.1016/j.jsp.2010.08.003

Sliwinski, M. J. (2008). Measurement-burst designs for social health research. *Social and Personality Psychology Compass*, *2*(1), 245–261. doi: https://doi.org/10.1111/j.1751-9004.2007.00043.x

Sliwinski, M. J. (2011). Approaches to modeling intraindividual and interindividual facets of change for developmental research. In K. L. Fingerman, C. A. Berg, J. Smith, & T. C. Antonucci (Eds.), *Handbook of lifespan research* (pp. 1–25). New York: Springer.

Sliwinski, M. J., Almeida, D. M., Smyth, J., & Stawski, R. S. (2009). Intraindividual change and variability in daily stress processes: Findings from two measurement-burst diary studies. *Psychology and Aging*, *24*(4), 828–840. doi: https://doi.org/10.1037/a0017925

Sliwinski, M. J., Hoffman, L., & Hofer, S. (2010). Modeling retest and aging effects in a measurement burst design. In P. C. M. Molenaar & K. M. Newell (Eds.), *Individual pathways of change: Statistical models for analyzing learning and development* (pp. 37–50). Washington, DC: American Psychological Association.

Smyth, J. M., Juth, V., Ma, J., & Sliwinski, M. (2017). A slice of life: Ecologically valid methods for research on social relationships and health across the life span. *Social and Personality Psychology Compass*, *11*(10), e12356. doi: https://doi.org/10.1111/spc3.12356

Spielberger, C. D., & Vagg, P. R. (1995). Test anxiety: A transactional process model. In C. D. Spielberger & P. R. Vagg (Eds.), *Series in clinical and community psychology. Test anxiety: Theory, assessment, and treatment* (pp. 3–14).Washington, DC: Taylor & Francis.

Stawski, R. S., MacDonald, S. W. S., & Sliwinski, M. J. (2016). Measurement burst design. In S. K. Whitbourne (Ed.), *The encyclopedia of adulthood and aging* (pp. 1–5). Hoboken, NJ: Wiley.

Steglich, C., Snijders, T. A. B., & Pearson, M. (2010). Dynamic networks and behavior: Separating selection from influence. *Sociological Methodology, 41* (1), 329–393. doi: https://doi.org/10.1111/j.1467-9531.2010.01225.x

Steiger, J. H. (1980). Tests for comparing elements of a correlation matrix. *Psychological Bulletin, 87,* 245–251. doi: https://doi.org/10.1037/0033-2909 .87.2.245

Sub, A., & Prabha, C. (2003). Academic performance in relation to perfectionism, test procrastination and test anxiety of high school children. *Psychological Studies, 48*(3), 77–81.

Sullivan, H. S. (1953). *The interpersonal theory of psychiatry.* New York: Norton.

Taber, K. S. (2018). The use of Cronbach's alpha when developing and reporting research instruments in science education. *Research in Science Education, 48* (6), 1273–1296. doi: https://doi.org/10.1007/s11165-016-9602-2

Terry, R. (2000). Recent advances in measurement theory and the use of sociometric techniques. *New Directions for Child and Adolescent Development,* 2000(88), 27–53. doi: https://doi.org/10.1002/cd.23220008805

Terry, R. & Coie, J. D. (1991). A comparison of methods for defining sociometric status among children. *Developmental Psychology, 27*(5), 867–880. doi: https://doi.org/10.1037/0012-1649.27.5.867

Thomas, H. J., Connor, J. P., & Scott, J. G. (2015). Integrating traditional bullying and cyberbullying: Challenges of definition and measurement in adolescents – a review. *Educational Psychology Review, 27*(1), 135–152. doi: https://doi.org/10.1007/s10648-014-9261-7

Tomada, G., & Schneider, B. H. (1997). Relational aggression, gender, and peer acceptance: Invariance across culture, stability over time, and concordance among informants. *Developmental Psychology, 33*(4), 601–609. doi: https:// doi.org/10.1037/0012-1649.33.4.601

Torabi, M. R. (1994). Reliability methods and numbers of items in development of health instruments. *Health Values: The Journal of Health Behavior, Education & Promotion, 18*(6), 56–59.

Veenstra, R., Dijkstra, J. K., Steglich, C., & Van Zalk, M. (2013). Network-behavior dynamics. *Journal of Research on Adolescence, 23*(3), 399–412. doi: https://doi.org/10.1111/jora.12070

Velásquez, A. M., Bukowski W. M., & Saldarriaga, L. M. (2013). Adjusting for group size effects in peer nomination data. *Social Development, 22*(4) 845–863. doi: https://doi.org/10.1111/sode.12029

Waldrip, A. M., Malcolm, K. T., & Jensen-Campbell, L. A. (2008). With a little help from your friends: The importance of high-quality friendships on Early

Adolescent Adjustment. *Social Development, 17*(4), 832–852. doi: https://doi.org/10.1111/j.1467-9507.2008.00476.x

Wigfield, A., & Eccles, J. S. (1989). Test anxiety in elementary and secondary school students. *Educational Psychologist, 24*(2), 159–183. doi: https://doi.org/10.1207/s15326985ep2402_3

Wine, J. (1971). Test anxiety and direction of attention. *Psychological Bulletin, 76*(2), 92–104. doi: https://doi.org/10.1037/h0031332

Wood, M. A., Bukowski, W. M., & Santo, J. B. (2017). Friendship security, but not friendship intimacy, moderates the stability of anxiety during preadolescence. *Journal of Clinical Child and Adolescent Psychology, 46* (6), 798–809. doi: https://doi.org/10.1080/15374416.2015.1094742

Woodgate, R. L., Tailor, K., Tennent, P., Wener, P., & Altman, G. (2020). The experience of the self in Canadian youth living with anxiety: A qualitative study. *PLOS ONE, 15*(1), e0228193. doi: https://doi.org/10.1371/journal.pone.0228193

Woodward, L. J., & Fergusson, D. M. (2001). Life course outcomes of young people with anxiety disorders in adolescence. *Journal of the American Academy of Child & Adolescent Psychiatry, 40*(9), 1086–1093. doi: https://doi.org/10.1097/00004583-200109000-00018

Zimmer-Gembeck, M. J. (2016). Peer rejection, victimization, and relational self-system process in adolescence: Toward a transactional model of stress, coping, and developing sensitivities. *Child Development Perspectives, 10*(2), 122–127. doi: https://doi.org/10.1111/cdep.12174

Acknowledgements

All authors significantly contributed to the preparation of this Element. Ryan J. Persram was responsible for the conceptualization of the project, oversaw the development each section, and wrote the general introduction and discussion. Bianca Panarello was responsible for the section on social and test anxiety. Melisa Castellanos was responsible for the section on the self-concept. Lisa Astrologo was responsible for the section on sociometric assessment. William M. Bukowski assisted with project conceptualization and data analyses, as well as contributed to each section within the Element. All of the authors were involved in reviewing and editing the Element. The authors acknowledge funding support from the Social Sciences and Humanities Research Council of Canada and the Fonds de Recherche du Québec: Société et Culture. We also wish to thank each of the schools, parents, principals, teachers, and students who participated in these studies. We are also grateful to members of the Interpersonal Relationships & Development laboratory, Gordon Rosenoff, Dr. Luz Stella Lopez, and Julie Brochero Paéz for their assistance with data collection and processing.

Cambridge Elements ☰

Research Methods for Developmental Science

Brett Laursen
Florida Atlantic University

Brett Laursen is a Professor of Psychology at Florida Atlantic University. He is Editor-in-Chief of the *International Journal of Behavioral Development*, where he previously served as the founding Editor of the Methods and Measures section. Professor Laursen received his Ph.D. in Child Psychology from the Institute of Child Development at the University of Minnesota and an Honorary Doctorate from Örebro University, Sweden. He is a Docent Professor of Educational Psychology at the University of Helsinki, and a Fellow of the American Psychological Association (Division 7, Developmental), the Association for Psychological Science, and the International Society for the Study of Behavioural Development. Professor Laursen is the co-editor of the *Handbook of Developmental Research Methods* and the *Handbook of Peer Interactions, Relationships, and Groups.*

About the Series

Each offering in this series will focus on methodological innovations and contemporary strategies to assess adjustment and measure change, empowering scholars of developmental science who seek to optimally match their research questions to pioneering methods and quantitative analyses.

Cambridge Elements ☰

Research Methods for Developmental Science

Elements in the Series

Measurement Burst Designs to Improve Precision in Peer Research
Ryan J. Persram, Bianca Panarello, Melisa Castellanos, Lisa Astrologo
and William M. Bukowski

A full series listing is available at: www.cambridge.org/ERMD

Printed in the United States
by Baker & Taylor Publisher Services